© Copyright 1986 by HAL LEONARD BOOKS
P.O. Box 13819, 8112 W. Bluemound Road
Milwaukee, WI 53213 U.S.A.

All rights reserved, which includes the right to reproduce this book or portions thereof in any form whatsoever except as provided by the U.S. Copyright Law.

Printed in the U.S.A.

Library of Congress Cataloging-in-publication Data

Brown, J. Aaron.
　　Sandi Patti : the book of words.

　　1. Patti, Sandi. 2. Singers—United States —Interviews. I. DeLaney, Kelly. II. Title.
ML420.P322B7 1986　784.5'0092'4 B　85-82507
ISBN 0-88188-463-4 (pbk.)

Produced & edited by J. Aaron Brown, Isabel D. Landeo & David R. Lehman

Designed by Teresa Towery and Ida Crosslin

Typeset by Karen Perry

Contributing articles by Kelly DeLaney, Gloria Gaither and Ron Patty

A
J. Aaron Brown & Associates, Inc.
Publication in association with

HAL LEONARD BOOKS

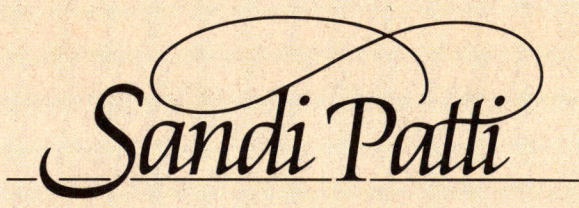

THE BOOK OF WORDS

CONTRIBUTING PHOTOGRAPHERS:
J. Aaron Brown, Bill Barnes, Mike Borum,
Don Boyer, Mark Johnson, David R. Lehman,
Ron Patty, Mark Tucker, Rich Voorhees

Special thanks to The Helvering Agency
for all project coordination with Ms. Patti.

CONTENTS

THE SONGWORDS INDEX — 6

FOREWORD BY RON PATTY (SANDI PATTI'S DAD) — 8

THE STORY — 11

"VIA DOLOROSA": FEATURE BY SANDI PATTI — 20

"MERRY CHRISTMAS WITH LOVE" FEATURE BY SANDI PATTI — 29

MY LIFE IS A SONG — 33

"IN THE NAME OF THE LORD" FEATURE BY SANDI PATTI — 59

A LIGHT TO A DARK WORLD — 76

MORE THAN MUSIC BY GLORIA GAITHER — 78

THE SONGWORDS INDEX

BECAUSE OF WHO YOU ARE by Billy Smiley & Bob Farrell — **22**
© Copyright 1982 by Paragon Music Corp./ASCAP. All Rights Reserved. International Copyright Secured.
Used by permission of The Benson Company, Inc., Nashville.

CRADLE SONG by Mark Gersmehl — **64**
© Copyright 1984 by Yellow House Music/ASCAP. All Rights Reserved. International Copyright Secured.
Used by permission of The Benson Company, Inc., Nashville.

FACE TO FAITH by Gary Driskell — **51**
© Copyright 1986 by StraightWay Music (ASCAP). All Rights Reserved. International copyright secured.
Used by permission. Administered by Gaither Music Company.

GIVE HIM THE GLORY by Brent Henderson & Steve Chapman — **23**
© Copyright 1984 by Paragon Music Corp./ASCAP., LifeSong Music Press/BMI, and Stych-n-Him Music/BMI.
All Rights Reserved. International Copyright Secured. Used by permission of The Benson Company, Inc., Nashville.

GLORIOUS MORNING by Lari Goss, Gary McSpadden & Linda Dooley — **74**
© Copyright 1984 by Songs of Promise (BMI), Kaanapali Music (ASCAP) and Ariose Music (ASCAP).
All rights reserved. International copyright secured. Used by permission.

GREAT IS THY FAITHFULNESS by Thomas O. Chisholm — **50**
© Copyright 1923. Renewal 1951 by Hope Publishing Company, Carol Stream, IL 60188.
All Rights Reserved. Used by Permission.

HOSANNA by Billy Smiley & Mark Gersmehl — **66**
© Copyright 1986 by Paragon Music Corp./ASCAP, and Bug and Bear Music/ASCAP.
All Rights Reserved. International Copyright Secured. Used By Permission.

HOW MAJESTIC IS YOUR NAME by Michael W. Smith — **31**
Copyright © 1981 Meadowgreen Music Co. All rights adm. by Tree Pub. Co., Inc. - 8 Music Sq. W., Nashville, TN 37203
International Copyright Secured   All Rights Reserved   Used By Permission

I'D RATHER HAVE JESUS by Rhea Miller & George Beverly Shea — **63**
© Copyright 1922, 1950. © Renewed 1939, 1966 by Chancel Music, Inc. Assigned to The Rodeheaver Co. (A Div. of WORD, INC.)
All Rights Reserved.   International Copyright Secured.   Used By Permission.

IN HIS HAND by Gary Chapman & Michael W. Smith — **75**
© Copyright 1980 by Paragon Music Corp./ASCAP. and Addi Music/BMI. All Rights Reserved.
International Copyright Secured. Used by permission of The Benson Company, Inc., Nashville.

IN HIS LOVE by Ed DeGarmo & Dana Key — **26**
© Copyright 1983 by Paragon Music Corp./ASCAP and Lion Cub Music/ASCAP.
All Rights Reserved. International Copyright Secured. Used by permission.

IN THE NAME OF THE LORD by Phill McHugh, Gloria Gaither & Sandi Patti Helvering — **58**
Copyright © 1986 River Oaks Music Co./Gaither Music Company/Sandi's Songs. River Oaks Music Co. adm. by Tree Pub. Co., Inc.
8 Music Sq. W., Nashville, TN 37203   International Copyright Secured   All Rights Reserved   Used By Permission

IT IS WELL WITH MY SOUL by Philip P. Bliss & Horatio G. Spafford — **62**
Public Domain

IT'S YOUR SONG, LORD by Billy Smiley, Claire Cloninger & Sandi Patti Helvering — **68**
© Copyright 1983 by Paragon Music Corp./ASCAP and Sandi's Songs/BMI.
All Rights Reserved. International Copyright Secured. Used by permission.

LET THERE BE PRAISE by Melodie Tunney & Dick Tunney — **24**
Copyright © 1985 Laurel Press, a division of Lorenz Creative Services/Pamela Kay Music/
Charlie Monk Music, Nashville, TN. International copyright secured. All rights reserved.

LIFT UP THE LORD by Billy Smiley, Gary McSpadden & Sandi Patti Helvering — **54**
© Copyright 1982 by Paragon Music Corp./ASCAP, Yellow House Music/ASCAP and Sandi's Songs/BMI.
All Rights Reserved. International Copyright Secured. Used by permission.

LOVE IN ANY LANGUAGE by Jon Mohr & John Mays **67**
© 1985 Jonathan Mark Music/Birdwing Music/Sutton Hill Music. Administered worldwide by
The Sparrow Corporation, 9255 Deering Ave., Chatsworth, CA 91311. All Rights Reserved. Used by Permission.

MERRY CHRISTMAS WITH LOVE by Billy Smiley & Greg Davis **28**
© Copyright 1984 by Paragon Music Corp./ASCAP. All Rights Reserved.
International Copyright Secured. Used by permission of The Benson Company, Inc., Nashville.

MORE THAN WONDERFUL by Lanny Wolfe **19**
© Copyright 1982 by Lanny Wolfe Music Company/ASCAP. All Rights Reserved.
International Copyright Secured. Used by permission of The Benson Company, Inc., Nashville.

POUR ON THE POWER by Mark Gersmehl, Niles Borop & Dwight Liles **30**
© Copyright 1984 by Paragon Music Corp./ASCAP, Word Music/ASCAP and Bug and Bear Music/ASCAP.
All Rights Reserved. International Copyright Secured. Used by permission.

PUREST PRAISE by Billy Smiley, Bill George & Scott Wesley Brown **53**
© Copyright 1984 by Paragon Music Corp./ASCAP, Yellow House Music/ASCAP and Laurel Press/ASCAP.
All Rights Reserved. International Copyright Secured. Used by permission.

SANDI'S SONG by Sandi Patti Helvering **61**
© Copyright 1979 by Singspiration (ASCAP), Division of the Zondervan Corporation. All rights reserved. Used by permission.

SHEPHERD OF MY HEART by Mark Baldwin & Dick Tunney **18**
Copyright © 1985 Laurel Press, a division of Lorenz Creative Services/Pamela Kay Music/
Charlie Monk Music, Nashville, TN. International copyright secured. All rights reserved.

SHINE DOWN by Billy Smiley, Mark Gersmehl & Bob Farrell **69**
© Copyright 1984 by Paragon Music Corp./ASCAP, Yellow House Music/ASCAP
and Efenbee Music/ASCAP. All Rights Reserved. International Copyright Secured. Used by permission.

SO FAR by Dawn Rodgers **25**
© Copyright 1980 by Paragon Music Corp./ASCAP. All Rights Reserved.
International Copyright Secured. Used by permission of The Benson Company, Inc., Nashville.

SOMEBODY BELIEVED by Gary Dunham & Rosemary Dunham **60**
© Copyright 1980 by LifeSong Music Press/BMI. All Rights Reserved.
International Copyright Secured. Used by permission of The Benson Company, Inc., Nashville.

THE STAGE IS BARE by Bill George, Sandi Patti Helvering, William J. Gaither, & Gloria Gaither **56**
© Copyright 1984 by Yellow House Music/ASCAP, Sandi's Songs/BMI and Gaither Music Co./ASCAP.
All Rights Reserved. International Copyright Secured. Used by permission.

THEY COULD NOT by Ron Harris & Claire Cloninger **57**
Copyright 1981, Ron Harris Music, All Rights Reserved, Used By Permission

UNSHAKABLE KINGDOM by Michael W. Smith, Gloria Gaither, Bill Gaither **27**
Copyright © 1984 Meadowgreen Music Co./Gaither Music Co. Meadowgreen Music Co. adm. by Tree Pub. Co., Inc.
8 Music Sq. W., Nashville, TN 37203   International Copyright Secured   All Rights Reserved   Used By Permission

UPON THIS ROCK by Gloria Gaither & Dony McGuire **55**
© Copyright 1983 by Gaither Music Company (ASCAP), Its-n-Me Music (ASCAP) and
Lexicon Music, Inc. (ASCAP). All rights reserved. International copyright secured. Used by permission.

VIA DOLOROSA by Billy Sprague and Niles Borop **21**
Copyright © 1983 Meadowgreen Music Co./Word Music Meadowgreen Music Co. adm. by Tree Pub. Co., Inc.
8 Music Sq. W., Nashville, TN 37203   International Copyright Secured   All Rights Reserved   Used By Permission

WAS IT A MORNING LIKE THIS by Jim Croegaert **70**
Copyright © 1978 Meadowgreen Music Co./Heart Of The Matter Music. All rights adm. by Tree Pub. Co., Inc.
8 Music Sq. W., Nashville, TN 37203   International Copyright Secured   All Rights Reserved   Used By Permission

WE SHALL BEHOLD HIM by Dottie Rambo **73**
© Copyright 1980 by John T. Benson Pub. Co./ASCAP. All Rights Reserved.
International Copyright Secured. Used by permission of The Benson Co., Inc., Nashville.

WHEN THE TIME COMES by David Kavich **71**
© Copyright 1981. New Spring Publishing, a member of Brentwood Publishing Group. All Rights Reserved.

YES, GOD IS REAL by Kenneth Morris **72**
© Copyright 1944 by Kenneth Morris, Martin & Morris Music, Inc., 4321 S. Indiana Avenue, Chicago, IL 60653

FOREWORD
by RON PATTY

As I look back on Sandi's life, and thinking of how words have affected her through the years, I can't believe how important words were in her development.

Even before Sandi was born, when her mother, Carolyn, was three months pregnant with our first child, I can still remember her suffering those hard labor pains of an impending miscarriage. Carolyn and I were in Chicago in the midst of a quartet tour when, early one morning in our hotel room, the pains became stronger and stronger. Carolyn called over to me and said, "Honey, please pray for me, I think I'm about to have a miscarriage." I can remember going to Carolyn, hugging her closely, and praying with a word, "Please!" And before I could even say, "Amen", Carolyn said, "Honey, the pains have stopped!" Then I sighed, "Thank you, God." I won't take time to tell them, but there were many other miracles connnected with Sandi finally making it into this world. Needless to say, every time I hear her sing, two words keep ringing through my mind: "Please" and "Miracle".

I also remember when Sandi was about two years old and was beginning to sing on a given pitch. She never was interested in singing "La-la-la" or other meaningless sounds, but was always wanting to sing with real words. Her first solo at two and a half years old was "Jesus Loves Me," those words have been the basis of Sandi's life ever since.

Another observation that comes to mind is that Sandi didn't play much with dolls because they couldn't respond to her words. "Why mess around with them when they don't respond to me?" was

Sandi's attitude. So we weren't surprised when Sandi, at age eight, answered the words of "Jesus Loves Me" with her words, "And I love You, Jesus!" She was going to respond even if no one else did.

Several interesting things happened in Sandi's high school days that reflected her deep feeling for communication. She hated then (and still dislikes) doing "dinner music" . . . singing or playing the piano while people eat and visit, paying little attention to the music. She has always felt that if she has something to say (or sing about) then she wanted the people to listen and hear the message. She would even take her own sound system (really MY system) while singing in high school groups so that the audience could more easily hear and understand the words. I can vividly recall her directing our church children's choir each week and hearing Sandi urging the kids to "sing on pitch" and "pronounce each word clearly".

The years have rolled on and by now, most people know about Sandi and her feel for the words and the message in each song. What they may not know is that every day, Sandi is studying God's Word, which tells about THE WORD MADE FLESH. This Word keeps reassuring Sandi of Jesus' never-ending love for her. I know of Jesus' love for Sandi, and am proud of Sandi's deep love for Him, and I am priviledged to write *these* few words about my daughter whom I love very much!

Ron Patty
(Sandi's Dad)

HE STORY

by KELLY DeLANEY

In one sense, Sandi Patti's singing career began literally by accident. In the winter of 1978 Sandi was a senior Music major at Indiana's Anderson College. She figured that after graduating and marrying John Helvering, her college sweetheart, she would settle down to a life as a music teacher.

Although she had been singing in churches virtually all of her life, first with her family's gospel group, and then on her own, she never planned to become a fulltime professional singer.

Still, she and John had discussed the possibility of her recording an album. However, there was one major stumbling block: They were two college kids who barely had enough money for a chocolate shake and two straws, let alone the cash it would take to record and press an album.

Then one winter day the answer came sliding down an ice-covered street and smashed into Sandi's parked car. Fortunately, the driver of the car which struck Sandi's vehicle was uninjured. And he was insured. His insurance covered the cost of the damage to Sandi's car. Through this fortunate accident Sandi had her album budget. "My car still ran fine, so we used the insurance money to pay for the album," she recalls.

And thus began the recording career of a woman who today is one of the finest vocalists in all of music. Attesting to her immense popularity in the Christian music field are the facts that her total record sales have exceeded three million units and that Sandi in a four-year period from 1982 to 1986, received 13 Dove Awards from The Gospel Music Association. In addition, she and Larnelle Harris teamed up for two Grammy Awards. Their duet recording of "More Than Wonderful" was honored as the Best Gospel Performance—Duo or Group in 1984. They won the same award in 1986 for their recording of "I've Just Seen Jesus."

In Gospel Music circles, Sandi, who possesses a three octave vocal range, is known as "The Voice." That voice has standardized such tunes as "Upon This Rock," "We Shall Behold Him," "More Than Wonderful," and "Via Dolorosa," all of which were Dove Award winning songs.

11

But sheer talent alone is not what makes Sandi such an acclaimed performer and recording artist. She is a woman who believes that the message contained in the songs she sings is far more important than the messenger who sings them. Her own life, both public and private, is a testimony to her faith. Despite her star status in contemporary Christian music, Sandi is first and foremost a Christian, a wife and a mother, and through her music, a friend and counsellor to all who hear her sing. Love, as much as talent, is the key to her success.

The oldest of three children, Sandi was born in Oklahoma City, where her father was a minister of music at a small church. When she was two-and-one-half-years-old, her father accepted a similar position at a church in Phoenix. On the last Sunday before her family moved to Arizona, Sandi sang her first song in public.

"It was a special music night at the church," she begins. "I sang 'Jesus Loves Me' before the congregation. I remember my Grandmother being in the audience and halfway through the song I stopped and said, 'Hi, Grandma!' Now that I have a child, I can understand how things like that happen."

The Patty family remained in Phoenix for some 10 years. "I remember a lot of things about Phoenix that played a part in my interest in music," Sandi says. "One was the children's choir and rhythm band that we had. I was very excited about that; we'd sing and put on little pageants."

When she was five-years-old Sandi sang at a mother-daughter banquet, accompanied by her Mother, who is an accomplished pianist. "She played and I sang a medley of rain songs," Sandi notes. "We had a screen set up, and I'd go behind it and change clothes very fast, put on a different hat, come out and sing another song. That was real fun."

Sandi also credits her elementary school music teacher for instilling her with a love for music. The woman, Mrs. Pat Rabé, was also a reason why Sandi wanted to become a teacher herself. "She, of all the teachers I had, was really the most influential in terms of music," Sandi adds. "She challenged us, but made it fun, too. I saw what an impact

she had on me, so I thought, 'Well, I have a desire to teach too, and share what I've learned."

When Sandi was about to enter junior high school the family moved once more. This time to San Diego, where her father continued his work as a minister of music. "There was always a lot of preparation going on around the house for what he was doing at the church," Sandi says. "My brothers and I took piano lessons, and every day after school we would come home and practice. My Mom would practice with us, but she sent us to another teacher because she thought we would be more serious about it if it was someone else we had to report to every week."

It was in San Diego, when her brothers were old enough, that the family began giving concerts in churches as The Ron Patty Family. Initially, most of their concerts were during summer vacations. "My Father booked all the concerts in churches across the country from San Diego to Indiana and back," Sandi explains. All five family members sang and accompanied themselves with piano, organ, bass and drums.

"I remember one year when my brother, Mike's voice was changing," Sandi giggles. "In the beginning of the year we had one set of vocal parts, but by the end of that year we all had to learn new parts because he couldn't sing his high part any more. Finally, when he had squeaked enough, we decided it was time to change."

With her family Sandi recorded several albums, including the first one, entitled *A Dream Come True*. "For my parents it really was a dream come true," she says. Her father, Ron, had once sang with Fred Waring and the Pennsylvanians, while her mother, Carolyn, had once been offered a contract as a concert pianist. Her parents met while they were both students at Anderson College.

As a teenager, Sandi was also influenced by the music of several secular artists. "When I was a sophomore in high school, I would get Karen Carpenter songbooks, sit down at the piano and sing the songs the way I thought Karen would sing them," Sandi says. "If I didn't get a part right, I would listen to the album to hear how she phrased it."

"As I got older, it became Barbra Streisand for me. I was so consumed by her music. I think a lot of that was good training. It has shaped so much of what I do now - the techniqes I've tried to incorporate into my style. One of the things about Barbra Streisand is that you always understood every word. That is something I learned from her - every word is there for a reason, so don't make any less of it."

Upon high school graduation, Sandi attended Anderson College for one semester, but then returned to San Diego to continue singing with the family group. By this time, 1975, her father had resigned his position as music minister, since The Ron Patty Family was receiving more concert requests. "For about a year-and-a-half we traveled and sang fulltime," Sandi adds.

She also attended classes at San Diego State University and worked as a teaching assistant at a local junior high school. After two-and-a-half years, she returned to Anderson College to complete her junior and senior years of school.

She met her future husband, John, through a music group, New Nature, which the college sponsored. "He was the sound engineer and I was one of the singers," Sandi reveals. "It was kind of a public relations group for the college. We traveled on weekends and during the summer. We spent a lot of time together and became good friends. Then, we thought, 'Hmm, there might be more to this!' "

In order to help pay for her college education, Sandi put her musical talents to work. She sang numerous commercial jingles, including one for Juicy Fruit Gum, worked as a background studio singer and taught piano lessons.

"About this time, my Mom and Dad were doing the music for the Bill Glass Crusades," Sandi continues. "They would also do concerts in some of the cities where the crusades were being held. So, I started joining them for those concerts. It seemed like maybe it was time to make an album by myself."

Not long after she and John reached this decision, the aforementioned "accident" occurred, providing them with the funds to record her first lp, appropriately entitled, *For My Friends*.

After graduation, she and John were married and continued living in Anderson. On weekends, Sandi would sing at church concerts and would have the album available for people to buy.

"I really didn't think anymore about it," notes Sandi. "We just continued doing what we were doing." However, a friend of hers, David Clydesdale, who still arranges some of the songs on Sandi's albums, gave a copy of *For My Friends* to the folks at Singspiration, a Christian record company. They signed Sandi to a recording contract and released her next album *Sandi's Song*.

Ironically, there was yet another "accident" in store for Sandi. During the printing of some promotional material, her last name was misspelled. Patty was misprinted as Patti. "Everyone thought it was real clever," laughs Sandi. "So I asked Mom and Dad if they cared.

Since they didn't mind, we left it that way."

Then in 1980, the Singspiration label merged with The Benson Company. On Benson's Impact label, she recorded her next album, *Love Overflowing*, which contained "We Shall Behold Him," now considered to be one of her signature songs.

It was also about this time that she became a featured vocalist with The Bill Gaither Trio. "I was singing at a music workshop and Bill Gaither happened to be there," Sandi says. "He had never really heard what I do. But a few weeks later he called and asked me if I would be interested in traveling with them, singing backup and doing a few of my own songs in their concerts. I said, 'Well, I really need to think about this - Yes!'"

Almost overnight, Sandi quadrupled her singing exposure through her work with the Gaithers. "I sang 'We Shall Behold Him' in their concerts," Sandi notes. "That song really got a lot of people's attention. Since I happened to be the one singing it, I kind of went along with the deal."

Sandi's own vocal talents, her appearances with The Bill Gaither Trio, and, of course, that classic Dottie Rambo tune, "We Shall Behold Him," all combined to propel Sandi into the thick of the Gospel Music Association's awards in 1982. That year she was nominated in two categories - Artist of the Year and Female Vocalist of the year. She swept both honors. Also, "We Shall Behold Him," which she sang, was voted Song of the Year.

Being a relative newcomer, she never expected to win the coveted Gospel Artist of the Year award. "It was really very surprising to us," she confides. "All we had done was sing 'We Shall Behold Him' around the country with The Bill Gaither Trio. When they announced my name, John and I both about passed out!"

For the next two years Sandi toured with the Gaither program. "One of the biggest things I learned from them is just simply be who you are," she says. "Don't try to be someone you're not when you're on stage. They are very genuine and they talk to the audience as if they were sitting in their living-room having coffee. I think the audience really felt that. I thought, 'You know, that's a lot easier than trying to be somebody else!'"

Finally, Sandi struck out on her own, first doing concerts in churches and

then progressing into larger auditoriums. John is also her personal manager and operates The Helvering Agency. "John has really been the one to have the vision for what we are doing," Sandi says. "There is nobody I would rather have represent me than my own husband. He is extremely supportive."

Both Sandi and John take their work seriously. "We've been very cautious, because we are sharing with people something that is vital," she explains. "We are sharing some life changing things, and you just don't take that lightly. You can't be flippant with that. It is my responsibility to make sure I am presenting things that I know to be true."

Through her music, Sandi actually is presenting a lifestyle. "I hope what I share in concert is a reflection of my life offstage," she says. "I want it to be an extension of what I am, rather than a total departure or a character that I am playing. Music is simply the form through which it is communicated."

But her musical ministry is not the only way through which Sandi communicates God's love. Offstage, in the wings of her life, Sandi also radiates a genuine concern for the spiritual wellbeing of others. Thus, when she realized she had a platform with young people, she formed The Friendship Company, a club for children up to age 12. The Friendship company is not a fan club intended to focus attention on Sandi. Instead, the focus is on the positive values found in God's word.

"I get a lot of letters from kids, and it got to the point where I couldn't answer all of them," Sandi says. "So, I thought, 'What could I do to take this interest and channel it? Kids are going to be drawn to somebody, and if at this point in their lives it happens to be me, what can I do to channel it toward Someone who is never going to change or let them down?'"

The result is The Friendship Company. Initially, Sandi thought maybe 400 children would join it. There are currently more than 25,000 youngsters in it.

"It doesn't cost the kids anything to be a part of it - except a smile," she says. "We give them a calendar with a different activity for each day. It might be something to think about, or it might be a real practical thing, like helping out around the house. We also send them a card on their birthday, and they can be

penpals with other members of the club. Some of them actually have met each other at our concerts, which is real neat."

Sandi also involves the children in her concerts by inviting them on stage to help her sing a song. Her own daughter, Anna, is also usually there to help her Mom sing. The sight of Sandi standing on stage with her own child, surrounded by other children, is, to say the least, inspiring.

Sandi is also sensitive to the needs of those less fortunate than herself. At about 25 percent of her concerts there now are deaf sections. She started signing the words to "We Shall Behold Him" out of consideration for the hearing impaired.

"I had gotten interested in that when I saw some other Christian artists use sign language on songs," she says. "It just made it come alive more for me. We started with 'We Shall Behold Him,' but I've learned more and more. My Dad says I always talk with my hands anyway, so I might as well make it mean something!"

And it does mean something, too. As an entire section of deaf people stands and signs the words to "We Shall Behold Him" along with Sandi, it is apparent that there is a transcendent depth of understanding which reveals the very heart of what faith and love are supposed to be all about. It is truly an unforgettable and beautiful sight as one realizes that the Word need never fall upon deaf ears.

"I want the music that I sing and the message that it brings, to challenge people into a deeper walk with the Lord, and into a better understanding and love for one another," she concludes.

Through her dedication and willingness to share her talent, Sandi is accomplishing her aim. She is indeed a teacher, a communicator, a guide who gently points the way.

Perhaps, Sandi Patti's music is no accident afterall.

SHEPHERD OF MY HEART

by Mark Baldwin & Dick Tunney

MAKER OF THIS HEART OF MINE
YOU KNOW ME VERY WELL
YOU UNDERSTAND MY DEEPEST PART
MORE THAN I KNOW MYSELF
SO WHEN I FACE THE DARKNESS
WHEN I NEED TO FIND MY WAY
I'LL TRUST IN YOU *SHEPHERD OF MY HEART*

KEEPER OF THIS HEART OF MINE
YOUR PATIENCE HAS NO END
YOU'VE LOVED ME BACK INTO YOUR ARMS
TIME AND TIME AGAIN
SO IF I START TO WANDER
LIKE A LAMB THAT'S GONE ASTRAY
I'LL TRUST IN YOU *SHEPHERD OF MY HEART*

YOU'RE THE BEACON OF MY NIGHTS
YOU'RE THE SUNLIGHT OF MY DAYS
I CAN REST WITHIN YOUR ARMS
I CAN KNOW YOUR LOVING WAYS
SO LET THE COLD WINDS BLOW
LET THE STORMS RAGE ALL AROUND
I'LL TRUST IN YOU *SHEPHERD OF MY HEART*

GIVER OF THIS LIFE IN ME
YOU'RE WHAT I'M LIVING FOR
FOR ALL MY DEEPEST GRATITUDE
YOU LOVE ME EVEN MORE
SO AS I WALK THROUGH VALLEYS
LISTENING FOR THE MASTER'S CALL
I'LL TRUST IN YOU *SHEPHERD OF MY HEART*

YOU'RE THE BEACON OF MY NIGHTS
YOU'RE THE SUNLIGHT OF MY DAYS
I CAN REST WITHIN YOUR ARMS
I CAN KNOW YOUR LOVING WAYS
SO AS I WALK THROUGH VALLEYS
LISTENING FOR THE MASTER'S CALL
I'LL TRUST IN YOU *SHEPHERD OF MY HEART*
I'LL TRUST IN YOU *SHEPHERD OF MY HEART*

MORE THAN WONDERFUL

by Lanny Wolfe

HE PROMISED US THAT HE WOULD BE A COUNSELOR
A MIGHTY GOD AND A PRINCE OF PEACE
HE PROMISED US
THAT HE WOULD BE A FATHER
AND HE WOULD LOVE US WITH A LOVE THAT WOULD NOT CEASE

WELL, I TRIED HIM
I FOUND HIS PROMISES ARE TRUE
HE'S EVERYTHING HE SAID THAT HE WOULD BE
THE FINEST WORDS I KNOW
COULD NOT BEGIN TO TELL
JUST WHAT JESUS REALLY MEANS TO ME

FOR HE'S MORE WONDERFUL
THAN MY MIND CAN CONCEIVE
HE'S MORE WONDERFUL
THAN MY HEART CAN BELIEVE
HE GOES BEYOND MY HIGHEST HOPES AND FONDEST DREAMS
HE'S EVERYTHING
THAT MY SOUL EVER LONGED FOR
EVERYTHING HE PROMISED AND SO MUCH MORE
HE'S MORE THAN AMAZING
MORE THAN MARVELOUS
MORE THAN MIRACULOUS COULD EVER BE
HE'S MORE THAN WONDERFUL
THAT'S WHAT JESUS IS TO ME

I STAND AMAZED WHEN I THINK THE KING OF GLORY
WOULD COME TO LIVE WITHIN THE HEART OF MAN
OH, I MARVEL JUST TO KNOW HE REALLY LOVES ME
WHEN I THINK OF WHO HE IS AND WHO I AM

FOR HE'S MORE WONDERFUL
THAN MY MIND CAN CONCEIVE
HE'S MORE WONDERFUL
THAN MY HEART CAN BELIEVE
HE GOES BEYOND MY HIGHEST HOPES AND FONDEST DREAMS
HE'S EVERYTHING
THAT MY SOUL EVER LONGED FOR
EVERYTHING HE PROMISED AND SO MUCH MORE
HE'S MORE THAN AMAZING
MORE THAN MARVELOUS
MORE THAN MIRACULOUS COULD EVER BE
HE'S MORE THAN WONDERFUL
THAT'S WHAT JESUS IS TO ME

"Not too long ago, we took a trip to Israel with The Gaither Trio, The Vocal Band and Larnelle Harris. We did a few concerts there, and we also spent a lot of time being good tourists. But for me it was so much more than sightseeing because we were walking the places that Jesus walked. We were seeing the places that He saw, and went to the mountainsides where He had given the sermon on the Mount and fed the five thousand—we visited the tomb *where He is no longer*.

"There was one place that especially intrigued me. It was just a very simple road, the road that goes from Jerusalem to Calvary. It was the road that Christ walked after He had been sentenced to be crucified. He had been beaten, He had been spat upon, He had been ridiculed, betrayed and denied. And he carried His own cross down the Via Dolorosa."

Via Dolorosa

by Niles Borop & Billy Sprague

DOWN THE *VIA DOLOROSA*
IN JERUSALEM THAT DAY
THE SOLDIERS TRIED TO CLEAR THE NARROW STREET
BUT THE CROWD PRESSED IN TO SEE
THE MAN CONDEMNED TO DIE ON CALVARY

HE WAS BLEEDING FROM A BEATING
THERE WERE STRIPES UPON HIS BACK
AND HE WORE A CROWN OF THORNS UPON HIS HEAD
AND HE BORE WITH EVERY STEP
THE SCORN OF THOSE WHO CRIED OUT FOR HIS DEATH

DOWN THE *VIA DOLOROSA*
CALLED THE WAY OF SUFFERING
LIKE A LAMB CAME THE MESSIAH
CHRIST THE KING
BUT HE CHOSE TO WALK THAT ROAD
OUT OF HIS LOVE FOR YOU AND ME
DOWN THE *VIA DOLOROSA*
ALL THE WAY TO CALVARY

POR LA *VIA DOLOROSA*
TRISTE DÍA EN JERUSALEM
LOS SOLDADOS LE ABRIÁN PASO A JESÚS
MAS LA GENTE SE ACERCABA
PARA VER AL QUE LLEVABA AQUELLA CRUZ

POR LA *VIA DOLOROSA*
QUE ES LA VIA DEL DOLOR
COMO OVEJA VINO CHRISTO
REY, SEÑOR
Y FUE EL QUIEN QUISO IR POR SU AMOR
POR TI Y POR MI
POR LA *VIA DOLOROSA*
AL CALVARIO Y A MORIR

THE BLOOD THAT WOULD CLEANSE THE SOULS OF ALL MEN
MADE IT'S WAY THROUGH THE HEART
OF JERUSALEM

DOWN THE *VIA DOLOROSA*
CALLED THE WAY OF SUFFERING
LIKE A LAMB CAME THE MESSIAH
CHRIST THE KING
BUT HE CHOSE TO WALK THAT ROAD
OUT OF HIS LOVE FOR YOU AND ME
DOWN THE *VIA DOLOROSA*
ALL THE WAY TO CALVARY

BECAUSE OF WHO YOU ARE

by Billy Smiley & Bob Farrell

YOU SPOKE THE WORDS AND ALL THE WORLDS CAME INTO ORDER
YOU WAVED YOUR HAND AND PLANETS FILLED THE EMPTY SKIES
YOU PLACED THE WOMAN AND THE MAN INSIDE THE GARDEN
AND THOUGH THEY FELL THEY FOUND COMPASSION IN YOUR EYES
OH LORD I STAND AMAZED AT THE WONDER OF YOUR DEEDS
AND YET A GREATER WONDER BRINGS ME TO MY KNEES

LORD I PRAISE YOU BECAUSE OF WHO YOU ARE
NOT JUST FOR ALL THE MIGHTY THINGS THAT YOU HAVE DONE
LORD I WORSHIP YOU BECAUSE OF WHO YOU ARE
YOU'RE ALL THE REASON THAT I NEED TO VOICE MY PRAISE
BECAUSE OF WHO YOU ARE

ONE HOLY NIGHT YOU BROUGHT YOUR PROMISE FROM A VIRGIN
AND PROMISE GREW AS HE REVEALED TO US YOUR HEART
ENDURING LOVE DISPLAYED THROUGHOUT HIS CRUCIFIXION
AND IN THE DARK YOU TORE THE GRAVE AND DEATH APART
OH LORD I STAND AMAZED AT THE WONDER OF YOUR DEEDS
AND YET A GREATER WONDER BRINGS ME TO MY KNEES

LORD I PRAISE YOU BECAUSE OF WHO YOU ARE
NOT JUST FOR ALL THE MIGHTY THINGS THAT YOU HAVE DONE
LORD I WORSHIP YOU BECAUSE OF WHO YOU ARE
YOU'RE ALL THE REASON THAT I NEED TO VOICE MY PRAISE
BECAUSE OF WHO YOU ARE

GIVE HIM THE GLORY

by Steve Chapman & Brent Henderson

LIFT YOUR VOICE AND SING
WE SERVE THE LIVING KING
OUR LIVES ARE THE THRONE
WHERE HIS GLORY SHONE
WILL DRAW ALL MEN TO JESUS

GIVE HIM THE GLORY
AND HONOR AND PRAISE
HE IS THE LORD OF CREATION ALWAYS
ALMIGHTY GOD
WORTHY ALONE TO BE PRAISED

LIFT YOUR EYES AND SEE
HIS POWER AND MAJESTY
OUR LIVES ARE THE THRONE
WHERE HIS GLORY SHONE
WILL DRAW ALL MEN TO JESUS

GIVE HIM THE GLORY
AND HONOR AND PRAISE
HE IS THE KING OF CREATION ALWAYS
ALMIGHTY GOD
WORTHY ALONE TO BE PRAISED

HE IS THE LORD
EVERY EYE WILL BEHOLD HIM
HE IS THE LORD
AND EVERY KNEE BOW IN PRAISE
HE IS THE LORD
EVERY TONGUE WILL CONFESS HIM
JESUS IS LORD
AND ALL THE EARTH WILL PROCLAIM
HE IS LORD

GIVE HIM THE GLORY
AND HONOR AND PRAISE
HE IS THE KING OF CREATION ALWAYS
ALMIGHTY GOD
WORTHY ALONE TO BE PRAISED

LET THERE BE PRAISE

by Dick Tunney & Melodie Tunney

LET THERE BE PRAISE
LET THERE BE JOY IN OUR HEARTS
FOREVERMORE
LET HIS LOVE FILL THE AIR
AND **LET THERE BE PRAISE**
LET THERE BE PRAISE
LET THERE, LET THERE BE PRAISE

LET THERE BE PRAISE
LET THERE BE JOY IN OUR HEARTS
SING TO THE LORD
GIVE HIM THE GLORY
LET THERE BE PRAISE
LET THERE BE JOY IN OUR HEARTS
FOREVERMORE
LET HIS LOVE FILL THE AIR
AND **LET THERE BE PRAISE**

HE INHABITS THE PRAISE OF HIS PEOPLE
AND DWELLS DEEP WITHIN
THE PEACE THAT HE GIVES NONE CAN EQUAL
HIS LOVE
IT KNOWS NO END
SO LIFT YOUR VOICES
WITH GLADNESS SING
PROCLAIM THROUGH ALL THE EARTH
THAT JESUS CHRIST IS KING

LET THERE BE PRAISE
LET THERE BE JOY IN OUR HEARTS
SING TO THE LORD
GIVE HIM THE GLORY
LET THERE BE PRAISE
LET THERE BE JOY IN OUR HEARTS
FOREVERMORE
LET HIS LOVE FILL THE AIR
AND **LET THERE BE PRAISE**

WHEN THE SPIRIT OF GOD IS WITHIN US
WE WILL OVERCOME
IN OUR WEAKNESS
HIS STRENGTH WILL DEFEND US
WHEN HIS PRAISE IS ON OUR TONGUE
SO LIFT YOUR VOICES
WITH GLADNESS SING
PROCLAIM THROUGH ALL THE EARTH
THAT JESUS CHRIST IS KING

AND **LET THERE BE PRAISE**
LET THERE BE SINGING
LET THERE BE MUSIC
LET THERE BE HONOR
LET THERE BE GLORY
MAJESTY, WORSHIP AND PRAISE
LET THERE BE PRAISE

SO FAR

by Dawn Rodgers

SO FAR
IT'S BEEN SO GOOD
SO FAR
THROUGH ALL THE JOYS AND SCARS
YOU'VE WON THE BATTLES IN MY HEART

I LONG
FOR WHAT YOU HAVE IN STORE
ANOTHER OPEN DOOR
SHOULD I STAY HERE OR LOOK FOR MORE

SO FAR
YOU'VE BROUGHT ME
SO FAR
YOU'VE TAUGHT ME
SO FAR
THAT EVERYTHING I NEED YOU ARE
AND NOW
ANOTHER TURN TO TAKE
ANOTHER CHOICE TO MAKE
I CAN'T BELIEVE WE'VE COME
SO FAR

YOU SAY
THE FIGHT HAS JUST BEGUN
AND YET THE BATTLE'S WON
BY TRUSTING IN YOUR HOLY SON

YOU KNOW
THE PLANS YOU HAVE FOR ME
I'M TRYING TO BELIEVE
BUT MY EYES CAN ONLY SEE SO FAR

SO FAR
YOU'VE BROUGHT ME
SO FAR
YOU'VE TAUGHT ME
SO FAR
THAT EVERYTHING I NEED YOU ARE
AND NOW
ANOTHER TURN TO TAKE
ANOTHER CHOICE TO MAKE
I CAN'T BELIEVE WE'VE COME
SO FAR

AND NOW
ANOTHER TURN TO TAKE
ANOTHER CHOICE TO MAKE
I CAN'T BELIEVE WE'VE COME
SO FAR

IN HIS LOVE

by Ed DeGarmo & Dana Key

IN HIS LOVE
THERE'S A PLACE WHERE YOU CAN
ALWAYS HIDE AWAY
IN HIS LOVE
THERE'S NO NEED TO RUN
NO NEED TO BE AFRAID
IF THE WORLD'S A SEA OF TROUBLE
YOU CAN ALWAYS RISE ABOVE
IF YOU KNOW THAT YOU ARE SAFELY
IN HIS LOVE

IN HIS LOVE
WHERE ALL PAIN AND SORROW
QUICKLY FADE AWAY
IN HIS LOVE
THERE'S A BRIGHT TOMORROW
JUST BEYOND TODAY
IF YOUR HEART IS FILLED WITH SORROW
IF IT'S ALL YOU CAN THINK OF
STILL THERE'LL BE A NEW TOMORROW
IN HIS LOVE

HIS LOVE IS NEVER FAR AWAY
YET SOMETIMES HARD TO SEE
IF WE WOULD TAKE THE TIME TO PRAY
HIS LOVE WOULD FLOW THROUGH YOU AND ME

IN HIS LOVE
THERE'S A PLACE WHERE YOU CAN
WATCH THE WORLD GO BY
IN HIS LOVE
THERE'S NO NEED TO HURRY
EVERYTHING'S ON TIME
WHEN THE WORLD'S A SEA OF TROUBLE
YOU CAN ALWAYS RISE ABOVE
IF YOU KNOW THAT YOU ARE SAFELY
IN HIS LOVE

IN HIS LOVE
THERE'S A PLACE WHERE YOU CAN
ALWAYS HIDE AWAY
IN HIS LOVE
THERE'S NO NEED TO RUN
NO NEED TO BE AFRAID
IF YOUR HEART IS FILLED WITH SORROW
IF IT'S ALL YOU CAN THINK OF
STILL THERE'LL BE A NEW TOMORROW
IN HIS LOVE

UNSHAKABLE KINGDOM

by Gloria Gaither, William J. Gaither & Michael W. Smith

THEY CAME TO FOLLOW HIM
DRAWN BY WHAT HE PROMISED THEM
IF THEY WOULD SELL ALL THAT THEY HAD
HE SAID THAT GOD WOULD SEND
A KINGDOM THAT WOULD NEVER END
WHERE ALL THE POOR WOULD BE SO RICH
AND IN THEIR DISCONTENT
THEY HEARD WHAT THEY THOUGHT HE MEANT
THEY HEARD THAT THE WEAK WOULD BE STRONG
BREAD WOULD BE MULTIPLIED
AND HUNGER BE SATISFIED
AND EVERY SERVANT A KING
IN THIS KINGDOM OF GOD
A KINGDOM THAT WOULD NEVER END
A LIVING *UNSHAKABLE KINGDOM* OF GOD

BUT HE WENT HIS QUIET WAY
GIVING HIMSELF AWAY
BUILDING WHAT EYES CAN NEVER SEE
WHILE MEN LOOKED FOR CROWNS AND THRONES
HE WALKED WITH CROWDS
ALONE
PLANTING A SEED IN YOU AND ME
CRYING FOR THOSE WHO CRIED
DYING FOR THOSE WHO DIED
BURSTING FORTH
GLORIFIED!
ALIVE!
AND SOME OF THEM LOOKED FOR HIM
SAD THAT IT HAD TO END
BUT SOME DARED TO LOOK WITHIN AND SEE

THE KINGDOM OF GOD
A KINGDOM THAT WILL NEVER END

THE LIVING
UNSHAKABLE KINGDOM OF GOD

STILL SOME OF US LOOK FOR HIM
SAD THAT IT HAS TO END
DO WE DARE TO LOOK WITHIN AND SEE
THE KINDGOM OF GOD
A KINDGOM THAT WILL NEVER END
THE LIVING
UNSHAKABLE KINGDOM OF GOD

MERRY CHRISTMAS WITH LOVE

by Billy Smiley & Greg Davis

SHE LEANED WITH HER HEAD ON THE WINDOW
WATCHING EVERGREEN BEND IN THE SNOW
REMEMBERING CHRISTMAS THE WAY IT HAD BEEN
SO MANY SEASONS AGO
WHEN THE CHILDREN WOULD REACH FOR THEIR STOCKINGS
AND OPEN THE PRESENTS THEY FOUND
THE LIGHTS ON THE TREE
WOULD SHINE BRIGHT IN THEIR EYES
REFLECTING THE LOVE ALL AROUND

BUT THIS YEAR THERE'S NO ONE TO OPEN THE GIFTS
NO REASON FOR TRIMMING THE TREE
AND JUST AS A TEAR MADE ITS WAY TO THE FLOOR
SHE HEARD VOICES OUTSIDE START TO SING

MERRY CHRISTMAS TO ALL WHO MAY DWELL HERE
MERRY CHRISTMAS IF EVEN JUST ONE
MAY THE JOY OF THE SEASON SURROUND YOU
MERRY CHRISTMAS WITH LOVE

THE CAROLERS SANG AS SHE OPENED THE DOOR
FACES OF FRIENDS IN THE CROWD
AND ALL OF THE SHADOWS OF LONELY REMINDERS WERE DRIVEN
AWAY BY THE SOUND
NOW THE HEART THAT FOR YEARS HAD BEEN SILENT
WAS SUDDENLY FILLED WITH A SONG
AS SHE CLUNG TO THEIR HANDS
LIKE A CHILD IN THE NIGHT
SHE FOUND HERSELF SINGING ALONG

MERRY CHRISTMAS TO ALL WHO MAY DWELL HERE
MERRY CHRISTMAS IF EVEN JUST ONE
MAY THE JOY OF THE SEASON SURROUND YOU
MERRY CHRISTMAS WITH LOVE

"When my family was living in Phoenix, every Christmas we would make our way to Sapulpa, Oklahoma where my Dad's family lived. Each year we looked forward to visiting my wonderful Grandma and Granpa Patty, all my cousins, aunts and uncles. It was terribly exciting for us because it would be snowing. Living in Phoenix, we weren't used to seeing snow.

"One Christmas my Mom and Dad just didn't feel like we had the money to make the trip back to Oklahoma. We were all a little disappointed because although we were glad to spend the time at home with just our family, it would be the first Christmas without our other relatives. The closer it got to Christmas, the more we began missing my Grandma and Granpa. So about two or three days before Christmas we decided to hop in the car and drive to Sepulpa and surprise everyone.

"We arrived on Christmas Eve and walked up the steps to the wooden porch that Grandma had at her house and started singing 'Joy to the World'. Grandma opened the door thinking that we were just carolers out on Christmas Eve and when she saw us standing there - I'll never forget the look on her face and the tears that came to her eyes. Of course the tears came to our eyes also and we knew we had made the right decision in coming to Sapulpa for Christmas.

"The thing that surprised me the most was that the next morning we woke up and there were presents under the tree for all of us. I remember thinking as a child, 'How did Santa know we were going to be at Grandma Patty's house for Christmas?' As I look back, I realize that all our relatives had scraped together some presents and wrapped them up for us that very same night. What a Christmas - so full of love!"

POUR ON THE POWER

by Mark Gersmehl, Niles Borop & Dwight Liles

LOOKING UP FROM THE BOTTOM
IT SEEMS LIKE A LONG WAY TO GO
THE MOUNTAIN'S DARK AND STEEP
THE CLIMBING IS OH SO SLOW
YOUR BODY ACHES
YOU'RE OUT OF BREATH
YOU'RE READY TO GIVE IN
BUT DON'T GIVE UP
YOU'VE GOT THE STRENGTH
TO MAKE IT TO THE END

YOU CAN *POUR ON THE POWER*
AND PULL THAT MOUNTAIN DOWN
POUR ON THE POWER
AND CLAIM THAT HIGHER GROUND
YOU MAY THINK YOU'RE AT A WALL
BUT IT'S JUST A DOOR THAT'S ALL
'CAUSE YOU AIN'T SEEN NOTHING
'TIL YOU *POUR ON THE POWER*
   (YOU GOTTA BELIEVE IT
      YOU GOTTA BELIEVE IT
         YOU GOTTA BELIEVE IT YOU CAN POUR ON THE POWER)

YOU DON'T HAVE TO BE WEARY
HIS POWER IS MOVING IN YOU
IF YOU'LL JUST DRAW UPON IT
YOU'RE STRENGTH'S GONNA BE RENEWED
THERE'S NO NEED TO TURN AROUND
THERE'S NO NEED TO STOP
STAND UP STRAIGHT
LOOK AHEAD
AND MARCH ON TO THE TOP

YOU CAN *POUR ON THE POWER*
AND PULL THAT MOUNTAIN DOWN
POUR ON THE POWER
AND CLAIM THAT HIGHER GROUND
YOU MAY THINK YOU'RE AT A WALL
BUT IT'S JUST A DOOR THAT'S ALL
'CAUSE YOU AIN'T SEEN NOTHING
'TIL YOU *POUR ON THE POWER*
   (YOU GOTTA BELIEVE IT
      YOU GOTTA BELIEVE IT
         YOU GOTTA BELIEVE IT YOU CAN POUR ON THE POWER)

WHEN IT'S HARD TO KEEP YOUR FEET ON THE ROAD
AND WHEN YOU NEED SOME HELP TO CARRY THE LOAD
JUST CALL UPON THE MASTER
AND YOU WILL RECEIVE
COURAGE AND STRENGTH THAT YOU NEED
TO BELIEVE

YOU CAN *POUR ON THE POWER*
AND PULL THAT MOUNTAIN DOWN
POUR ON THE POWER
AND CLAIM THAT HIGHER GROUND
YOU MAY THINK YOU'RE AT A WALL
BUT IT'S JUST A DOOR THAT'S ALL
'CAUSE YOU AIN'T SEEN NOTHING
NO YOU AIN'T SEEN NOTHING
'TIL YOU *POUR ON THE POWER*
   (YOU GOTTA BELIEVE IT
      YOU GOTTA BELIEVE IT
         YOU GOTTA BELIEVE IT YOU CAN POUR ON THE POWER)

HOW MAJESTIC IS YOUR NAME

by Michael W. Smith

OH LORD, OUR LORD
HOW MAJESTIC IS YOUR NAME
IN ALL THE EARTH
OH LORD, OUR LORD
HOW MAJESTIC IS YOUR NAME
IN ALL THE EARTH

OH LORD, WE PRAISE YOUR NAME
OH LORD, WE MAGNIFY YOUR NAME
PRINCE OF PEACE
MIGHTY GOD
OH LORD GOD ALMIGHTY

OH LORD, OUR LORD
HOW MAJESTIC IS YOUR NAME
IN ALL THE EARTH
OH LORD, OUR LORD
HOW MAJESTIC IS YOUR NAME
IN ALL THE EARTH

OH LORD, WE PRAISE YOUR NAME
OH LORD, WE MAGNIFY YOUR NAME
PRINCE OF PEACE
MIGHTY GOD
OH LORD GOD ALMIGHTY

OH LORD, OUR LORD
HOW MAJESTIC IS YOUR NAME
IN ALL THE EARTH
OH LORD, OUR LORD
HOW MAJESTIC IS YOUR NAME
IN ALL THE EARTH

OH LORD, WE PRAISE YOUR NAME
OH LORD, WE MAGNIFY YOUR NAME
OH LORD, WE PRAISE YOUR NAME
OH LORD, WE MAGNIFY YOUR NAME
PRINCE OF PEACE
MIGHTY GOD
OH LORD GOD ALMIGHTY

PRINCE OF PEACE
MIGHTY GOD
OH LORD GOD ALMIGHTY
WE MAGNIFY YOUR NAME

MY LIFE IS A SONG

by KELLY DeLANEY

Sandi Patti loves to sing, and what she sings about is love. It is the one constant ingredient in all her music. If a song does not in some way convey love of God or of fellow human beings, she simply chooses not to record or sing it.

Perhaps this is what makes her such a unique recording artist. A song's commercial value alone is virtually of no importance to her. Sandi's primary concern is that a song have a positive message which somehow draws the listener closer to God or to other people.

Sandi's albums are the result of abundant planning and thought. With the assistance of co-producer, Greg Nelson, she spends countless hours screening material before narrowing down the hundreds of submissions to the 10 tunes which make it onto an album.

"Most of the songs are sent to me or to Greg," she explains. "We always read the lyrics first because that's really what is important to us - that it say something. Then we listen to the music, and if it complements the lyrics, then you've got a good song."

Although many of the tunes submitted to her for consideration are sparse, piano-vocal demos, some songs actually are demoed with a band, making for a fuller, more comprehensible sound. "Good quality demos really help in the evaluation of songs," she advises.

While Sandi's albums ultimately revolve around a particular concept, as is the case with her *Morning Like This* lp, ironically they don't start out that way. The concept develops from the songs themselves as they are chosen.

"We get 25 or 30 songs that are good contenders," she says. "Then we make sure we have enough balance - enough uptempo songs and all that; what does it say? Is there another song that says the same kind of thing? We come up with 10 that go together well and are comfortable to sing and hear."

Songs can be as memorable and meaningful to Sandi as they can be to the listeners. Songs can crystalize certain past moments in one's life or evoke feelings deep in the heart and soul. Sandi has an intuitive grasp of these qualities in songs. In their own distinct way all the songs Sandi has ever recorded are special to her. Within the broad meaning of a song there are many interpretations. There is a personal side to many of the songs Sandi records.

For example, there is the self-penned "Sandi's Song". "One day I was sitting at my piano in the livingroom, just kind of tinkering around like I do sometimes when there's something on my mind," she begins. "And this particular day I found myself leafing through the hymnal that was sitting on the piano and looking at all of the songs that had been written to our Lord, thanking Him for His faithfullness, praising Him for His goodness, and I wished that I could write a song to express to

the Lord the way that I felt about Him."

As she sat at her piano, the song developed spontaneously in much the same way that one offers up a personal prayer to the Creator. "Really, I just started talking to Him and telling Him what I was feeling, not in fancy words, not in clever cliches, but just simply words from my heart, and I wrote a song for Him," she says.

Another very personal song for her is "When The Time Comes," which is contained on both her *Live, More Than Wonderful* and *Love Overflowing* lps. The live album was dedicated to her dear friend, Debbie Cleary who was killed in a tragic automobile accident. Initially, Debbie was going to sing on that album with Sandi.

"She was the sort of person you could meet for the first time, and after the first five minutes you felt like you knew her," Sandi says. "Debbie and I had a lot in common. We sang together; we liked to laugh together; and we went to Weight Watchers together! I would call her and say, 'I've been thinking about this problem and I think the only solution is a banana split.' And Debbie would say, 'Sandi, in our weakness, He is strong,'"

Debbie's death, as tragic and seemingly untimely as it was, forced Sandi to think about her own life and its priorities. "God has given us many special friends," Sandi offers. "Maybe we need to hug them a little more often and tell them that we love them. Because when the time comes for me, I want my friends and family to know I love them and I want to know I have been loved."

Some songs even recall childhood memories, as is the case with "Give Him The Glory" from her *Songs From The Heart* album. "Ever since I was eight-years-old and my brother, Michael was six and my brother, Craig was three, we all sang together," she says. "We had a little trio - The Patty Kids. We have continued to sing together, so when we did this song, I wanted very much to include my brothers. Nobody else - just my two brothers and myself to do a trio part like we had done at different times in our lives. And that's what makes this song special to me."

Since the birth of her first child, Anna, Mark Gersmehl's "Cradle Song" has taken on a particularly personal meaning. "I cannot remember a time in my life when I did not want to be a mother," Sandi confides. "Becoming a mother is something that I have looked forward to, I think, ever since I played with my first doll. When the time came for John and I to add to our family, we were very excited and very thankful that God had allowed us to be in charge of a little life for a few years on earth."

Originally, the song was a Christmas present from the writer to Sandi and John. "It was written for us in honor of our first, as yet unborn child," Sandi reveals. "It was given to us the Christmas before Anna was born. She was born May 22, 1984 and she has brought us so much joy. The song is very special, and the way that it came to us makes it even more special. Thanks, Mark."

A number of the songs Sandi has recorded have resulted in award-winning performances. Her duet with Larnelle Harris, "More Than Wonderful," is one of the most celebrated recordings in recent Christian music history. It earned them both a Grammy and a Dove Award. The song is part of a musical - "Thou Shalt Call His Name...Jesus," written by Lanny Wolfe.

As impossible as it may sound, the first time Sandi and Harris recorded it as a duet, they didn't sing it together. "Lanny and his arranger, Don Marsh, began talking about who might work well together to sing that duet, and my name and Larnelle's came up," Sandi says. "At the time, I had never met Larnelle before. I had certainly been familiar with his work and I was a great admirer of his, but I had never met him."

Although they tried to arrange their busy schedules to a convenient time when they could both be in the studio to sing the song together, they were unable to do so.

"So, what happened was Larnelle went into the studio and did his part on 'More Than Wonderful' for the musical (sound track album) and a couple of weeks later, I went in and sang my part," Sandi explains.

Even though they did not sing at the same time, their vocal tracks displayed their harmonious musical chemistry. "He had done some phrasing that was very natural for me," Sandi notes. "In fact, I probably would have interpreted it that way myself.

There was just a real compatability between us."

Hence, when Sandi decided to record her live album, she invited Harris to sing "More Than Wonderful" with her. "We thought that might be just the perfect little extra surprise," she adds.

(It should be noted that she and Harris have recorded a song on each other's albums. After "More Than Wonderful," Sandi returned the favor by singing "I've Just Seen Jesus" with Harris on his album. Both songs have won Grammy awards.)

Another important song in Sandi's career is the Dottie Rambo evergreen, "We Shall Behold Him." It's the song which really launched her career in earnest. Sandi has recorded it twice - once on her live album and previously on the *Love Overflowing* lp.

In concert Sandi sings the words to this song so that deaf people who attend her performances, can, in a sense, hear the words to this beautiful tune. "I remember one concert, I'm not exactly sure where we were, but it was a very special concert," she says. "It was one of those concerts where there was a real special feeling throughout the whole evening. At this particular concert there was a deaf section, and they had an interpreter who was signing the entire concert for them.

I had been very fascinated by sign language and the whole idea of comunicating with people in a way that they can understand. When we got to the end of the concert, I sang 'We Shall

Behold Him,' which I had learned to sign. I started signing the song and the interpreter sat down. I looked over to the deaf section and they were all standing, signing with me."

The sight was an emotional experience for Sandi. "I was reminded of the scripture that on that day 'every eye will see, every knee will bow, every tongue will confess'," **she says.** "And, I even think that every ear will hear that Jesus Christ is the King of kings and Lord of lords."

Occasionally, there are songs which have stories all their own. That is the case with "It Is Well With My Soul," which Sandi recorded on her *Hymns...Just For You* album. Written in the early 1900s, the song was inspired out of a tragedy.

"Horatio Stafford, a wealthy Chicago businessman, lived there with his wife and four daughters," **Sandi relates.** "His wife decided to take an overseas trip with her daughters. While they were at sea, a fierce storm developed, resulting in a terrible shipwreck. All four daughters were killed, but Mrs. Stafford survived. She sent a wire to her husband which stated, 'Saved alone.'

"Horatio immediately took the next available ship to meet his wife. During the trip he asked the captain to have someone notify him when they reached the location where the other ship had wrecked. When he came to the place, Horatio walked out onto the balcony and wrote the words to 'It Is Well With My Soul,' which began, 'When peace like a river attendeth my

way, When sorrows like sea billows roll; Whatever my lot, Thou hast taught me to say, It is well, it is well with my soul.' Later, Phillip Bliss set the lyrics to music."

One of the most inspiring songs Sandi has ever recorded is "Face To Faith," on her *Morning Like This* lp. The song has an inner strength and a sense of indomitable courage which can be utilized in life's many battles. It has this effect on Sandi, too.

"I have very much felt like David," she says. "It's those times when I'm coming up against a giant in my life and I don't feel like I have the weapons to overcome that giant. David didn't have all the latest equipment; he didn't have a fancy sword or helmet. All he had was what he knew how to use best. He had a sling, so he picked up a rock. He also had very good aim, and he knew right where the giant's weakness was. God used what David had and gave him the courage to meet that giant face to faith."

"In my own life I sometimes may feel like I don't have all the latest things to tackle that giant, but through faith I have the right equipment. With good aim I can hit that giant square in the head. When I come up to my giant, it's face to faith,"

But the one song which possibly capsulizes the essence of Sandi and her music is also from her *Morning Like This* album - "Love In Any Language."

"A hobby of mine has always been the study of foreign languages," she says. "When I was in college, I studied French and Spanish, and whenever our travels would take us to a foreign country I would learn a song in that language. When we were in Indonesia, I learned 'How Great Thou Art' in Indonesian. And when we were in Israel, I learned some songs in Hebrew."

It occurred to Sandi that there is indeed one absolute in all Divine and human relationships. "The amazing thing to me is that no matter how you may say something, no matter which language you may use, the meaning seems to always stay the same," she suggests. "You can never change the meaning of love, although the ways to say love may be different. A smile never changes, childrens' laughter never changes, and neither does the love that God has for us, or that genuine love from Him that we show to others. And so, no matter what language we say love in, when it comes from the heart, it is never misunderstood."

There is also no misunderstanding why Sandi Patti has chosen to sing. She's not only filling hearts with song; she's filling them with love as well.

GREAT IS THY FAITHFULNESS

by T.O. Chisolm

GREAT IS THY FAITHFULNESS
GREAT IS THY FAITHFULNESS
MORNING BY MORNING
NEW MERCIES I SEE
ALL I HAVE NEEDED
THY HAND HATH PROVIDED
GREAT IS THY FAITHFULNESS
LORD UNTO THEE

GREAT IS THY FAITHFULNESS, O GOD MY FATHER
THERE IS NO SHADOW OF TURNING WITH THEE
THOU CHANGEST NOT
THY COMPASSIONS THEY FAIL NOT
AS THOU HAST BEEN THOU FOREVER WILT BE

SUMMER AND WINTER AND SPRINGTIME AND HARVEST
SUN, MOON, AND STARS IN THEIR COURSES ABOVE
JOIN WITH ALL NATURE
IN MANIFOLD WITNESS
TO THY GREAT FAITHFULNESSS, MERCY AND LOVE

PARDON FOR SIN AND A PEACE THAT ENDURETH
THY OWN DEAR PRESENCE TO CHEER AND TO GUIDE
STRENGTH FOR TODAY
AND BRIGHT HOPE FOR TOMORROW
BLESSINGS ALL MINE, WITH TEN THOUSAND BESIDE

FACE TO FAITH

by Gary Driskell

DAVID WAS SMALL, BUT NO GIANT COULD TAKE HIM
DANIEL WAS DOOMED, BUT THERE WAS NOT A WOUND
    WHEN THEY RAISED HIM FROM THE LION'S DEN
SIMON PETER, IN CHAINS, BROUGHT AN ANGEL TO THE RESCUE
PAUL AND SILAS, IN JAIL, WERE GUARDED TO NO AVAIL
    FOR THEIR SHACKLES WERE LOOSE, AND THE DOORS
    JUST FLEW OPEN
"WHAT IS THE CATCH?" I ASKED ONE DAY I WAS READIN'
IT MUST BE AN AGE OLD MYSTERY
THEN, TAKIN' A SECOND LOOK
I DISCOVERED A STRIKINGLY CLEAR CONSISTENCY

IT'S MEETIN' DISASTER FACE TO FAITH
PUTTIN' GOD'S PROMISES INTO PLACE
TENDIN' TO TROUBLE WITH A LITTLE TASTE
    OF WHAT GOD WILL DO WHEN HIS PEOPLE START
    CALLIN' ON HIS NAME
FOR HE ANXIOUSLY AWAITS TO GIVE THE WORD
    TO RELEASE THE POWER
THAT PRAYER CREATES SO WE'VE GOTTA LEARN TO MEET
    EVERY PROBLEM THAT WE FACE
FACE TO FAITH

NOW, NOW, NOW, NOW, PEOPLE, I'VE LEARNED
    THAT GOD'S WORD CAN BE TESTED
JUST TRUST HIM, YOU'LL SEE, FOR THOSE WHO BELIEVE
    HE'S STILL A GOD OF MIGHTY MIRACLES
SO WHEN TROUBLES HIT HARD TURN TO
    GOD AND BE PATIENT
STAND STRONG, DON'T RUN, FOR THERE ISN'T
    ANYONE THAT HE'S EVER LET DOWN WHEN THEIR
    LIVES HAVE BEEN FAITHFUL
IT'S EASY TO GO HALF-WAY AND NOT REALLY DO IT
BUT THAT MAKES THE CONSEQUENCES ROUGH
AND THE MORE THE CATASTROPHE
THE SOONER YOU SEE THAT YOU'RE SO MUCH
    BETTER OFF

IT'S MEETIN' DISASTER FACE TO FAITH
PUTTIN' GOD'S PROMISES INTO PLACE
TENDIN' TO TROUBLE WITH A LITTLE TASTE
    OF WHAT GOD WILL DO WHEN HIS PEOPLE START
    CALLIN' ON HIS NAME
FOR HE ANXIOUSLY AWAITS TO GIVE THE WORD
    TO RELEASE THE POWER
THAT PRAYER CREATES SO WE'VE GOTTA LEARN TO MEET
    EVERY PROBLEM THAT WE FACE
FACE TO FAiTH

HE WILL DELIVER US
IF WE ONLY LEARN TO TRUST

MEETIN' DISASTER FACE TO FAITH
WE GOTTA START MEETIN' DISASTER FACE TO FAITH
MEETIN' DISASTER FACE TO FAITH
WE GOTTA START MEETIN' DISASTER FACE TO FAITH
FACE TO FAITH

PUREST PRAISE

by Bill George, Scott Wesley Brown & Billy Smiley

PRAISE HIM, PRAISE HIM
ALL YE LITTLE CHILDREN
GOD IS LOVE, GOD IS LOVE
PRAISE HIM, PRAISE HIM
ALL YE LITTLE CHILDREN
GOD IS LOVE, GOD IS LOVE

LISTEN TO THE PUREST PRAISES
AS YOU HEAR THE LITTLE CHILDREN SING
WE ARE CHILDREN OF ALL AGES
JOIN OUR VOICES AS WE PRAISE THE KING
SONG OF GLORY
SONG OF CELEBRATION
SINGING GLADLY
JESUS WE ADORE
CELEBRATING AS A FAMILY
ALL GOD'S CHILDREN
SING UNTO THE LORD

SING ALL OF YE CHILDREN SING
YOUNG AND OLD IN ONE ACCORD
SING ALL OF YE CHILDREN SING
A NEW SONG BEFORE HIM, ADORE HIM
LET ALL THE NATIONS PRAISE HIM
KNEELING BEFORE THE LORD MOST HIGH

LET THE CHILDREN'S SONG ARISE
FULL OF JOY AND WONDER FROM ABOVE
WE ARE CHILDREN IN GOD'S EYES
SINGING PRAISES ECHOING GOD'S LOVE
SONG OF GLORY
SONG OF CELEBRATION
SINGING GLADLY
JESUS WE ADORE
CELEBRATING AS A FAMILY
ALL GOD'S CHILDREN
SING UNTO THE LORD

SING ALL OF YE CHILDREN SING
YOUNG AND OLD IN ONE ACCORD
SING ALL OF YE CHILDREN SING
A NEW SONG BEFORE HIM, ADORE HIM
LET ALL THE NATIONS PRAISE HIM
KNEELING BEFORE THE LORD MOST HIGH

PUREST PRAISE COMES FROM THE HEART
AND THE LORD IS GLORIFIED
LET ALL THE PEOPLE PRAISE HIM
KNEELING BEFORE THE LORD MOST HIGH

SING ALL OF YE CHILDREN SING
YOUNG AND OLD IN ONE ACCORD
SING ALL OF YE CHILDREN SING
A NEW SONG BEFORE HIM, ADORE HIM
LET ALL THE PEOPLE PRAISE HIM
KNEELING BEFORE THE LORD MOST HIGH
LET ALL THE NATION'S PRAISE HIM
KNEELING BEFORE THE LORD MOST HIGH

LIFT UP THE LORD

by Billy Smiley, Gary McSpadden, & Sandi Patti Helvering

THIS IS THE PLACE AND THE LORD IS HERE
HIS LOVE IS ALL WE NEED
LIFT YOUR VOICE AND SING THIS SONG
THE SONG OF THE REDEEMED

LET'S CELEBRATE AND JOIN OUR HANDS
LIFTING UP OUR KING
LOVING ONE ANOTHER HERE
HIS LOVE IS WHAT WE BRING

LIFT UP THE LORD
RIGHT HERE WHERE WE ARE
LIFT UP THE LORD
FOR LOVING US AND BRINGING US THIS FAR

THE TIME IS RIGHT AND WE HAVE COME
TO GLORIFY HIS NAME
IF WE OPEN UP TO HIM
WE WON'T LEAVE HERE THE SAME

THERE IS NOTHING WE CAN'T DO
WITH HIS POWER AND MIGHT
LET'S SHOW HIS LOVE TO ALL THE WORLD
WE'RE CALLED TO BE HIS LIGHT

LIFT UP THE LORD
RIGHT HERE WHERE WE ARE
LIFT UP THE LORD
FOR LOVING US AND BRINGING US THIS FAR

I DON'T KNOW WHAT BROUGHT YOU HERE
BUT I'M SO GLAD YOU CAME
TO HELP ME LIFT THIS SONG OF PRAISE
AND MAGNIFY HIS NAME

LIFT UP THE LORD
RIGHT HERE WHERE WE ARE
LIFT UP THE LORD
FOR LOVING US AND BRINGING US THIS FAR

LIFT UP THE LORD

UPON THIS ROCK

by Gloria Gaither & Dony McGuire

WHEN OTHERS SEE WITH EARTHLY EYES
JUST WHAT THEY WANT TO SEE
YOU WILL SEE THE THINGS THAT NEVER DIE
YOU WILL KNOW AND RECOGNIZE
BY SIMPLE CHILD-LIKE FAITH
THE PRICELESS TRUTH OTHERS WILL DENY

   WHEN OTHERS SAY I'M JUST A MAN
   WHO LIKES TO DREAM HIS DREAMS
   WHEN OTHERS CALL A MIRACLE A MYTH
   YOU LISTEN FOR ETERNITY
   IN MOMENTS AS THEY PASS
   AND SEE WITH SPIRIT EYES WHAT OTHERS MISS

UPON THIS ROCK
I'LL BUILD MY KINGDOM
AND ON THIS ROCK
FOREVER AND EVER IT SHALL STAND
AND ALL THE POWERS OF HELL ITSELF
SHALL NEVER MORE PREVAIL AGAINST IT
FOR SATAN'S THRONES ARE BUILT ON SINKING SAND
UPON THIS ROCK
I'LL BUILD MY KINGDOM
AND ON THIS ROCK
FOREVER AND EVER IT SHALL STAND
UPON THIS ROCK OF REVELATON
I'LL BUILD A STRONG AND MIGHTY NATION
AND IT SHALL STAND THE STORMS OF TIME
UPON THIS ROCK

   IF IN A SIMPLE CARPENTER
   YOU SEE THE SON OF GOD
   IF YOU WOULD CHOOSE TO LOSE
   WHEN YOU COULD WIN
   IF YOU WOULD GIVE YOUR LIFE AWAY
   FOR NOTHING IN RETURN
   THEN YOU ARE WHERE MY KINGDOM WILL BEGIN

UPON THIS ROCK
I'LL BUILD MY KINGDOM
AND ON THIS ROCK
FOREVER AND EVER IT SHALL STAND
AND ALL THE POWERS OF HELL ITSELF
SHALL NEVER MORE PREVAIL AGAINST IT
FOR SATAN'S THRONES ARE BUILT ON SINKING SAND
UPON THIS ROCK
I'LL BUILD MY KINGDOM
AND ON THIS ROCK
FOREVER AND EVER IT SHALL STAND
UPON THIS ROCK OF REVELATON
I'LL BUILD A STRONG AND MIGHTY NATION
AND IT SHALL STAND THE STORMS OF TIME

   UPON THIS ROCK
   I'LL BUILD MY KINGDOM
   AND ON THIS ROCK
   FOREVER IT SHALL STAND
   UPON THIS ROCK OF REVELATION
   I'LL BUILD A STRONG AND MIGHTY NATION
   AND IT SHALL STAND THE STORMS OF TIME
   UPON THIS ROCK
   I'LL BUILD MY CHURCH
   UPON THIS ROCK

THE STAGE IS BARE

by Gloria Gaither, William J. Gaither, Bill George & Sandi Patti Helvering

THE STAGE IS BARE
THE CROWDS ARE GONE
THE LOVE WE SHARED
STILL LINGERS ON
WE SANG AND PLAYED
AND WE LAUGHED AND CRIED
AND IN OUR FUMBLING WAY WE TRIED TO SAY
WHAT ONLY HEARTS CAN KNOW
AND ALL TOO SOON WE HAD TO GO
BUT NOW HERE IN THIS DARKENED ROOM
JUST EMPTY SEATS THERE'S JUST ME...AND YOU
IT WAS EASY TO CALL YOU "LORD"
WHEN A THOUSAND VOICES SANG YOUR PRAISE
BUT THERE'S NO ONE TO HEAR ME NOW
SO HEAR ME NOW...BE NEAR ME NOW

THE STAGE IS BARE
THE CROWDS ARE GONE
LORD, NOW'S THE TIME I NEED YOUR SONG
TO GIVE ME JOY AND CERTAINTY
WHEN NO ONE ELSE IS WATCHING ME
I NEED YOU MORE THAN WORDS CAN SAY
TOMORROW'S SUCH A DAILY DAY
AND I SO NEED TO FEEL YOU THEN
HOLDING MY HAND
PLEASE HOLD ME THEN

THEY COULD NOT

by Ron Harris & Claire Cloninger

THEY LOOKED AT HIM AND SAW A SIMPLE MAN
A CARPENTER WITH HEALING IN HIS HANDS
THEY SAW HIM CALM THE SEA
AND HEAL A DYING MAN
THEY SAW BUT COULD THEY REALLY UNDERSTAND

*THEY COULD NOT
THEY COULD NOT
THOUGH THEY TRIED
THEY COULD NOT
HE WAS JUST A SIMPLE CARPENTER
WITH HEALING IN HIS HANDS
BUT COULD THEY REALLY UNDERSTAND
THEY COULD NOT*

THEY LISTENED TO THE TEACHING THAT THEY'D HEARD
THEY WONDERED AT THE MYSTERY OF HIS WORD
THEY WONDERED WHAT HE MEANT ABOUT A FATHER'S PLAN
THEY HEARD BUT COULD THEY REALLY UNDERSTAND

*THEY COULD NOT
THEY COULD NOT
THOUGH THEY TRIED
THEY COULD NOT
THEY LISTENED TO THE TEACHING
ABOUT A FATHER'S PLAN
BUT COULD THEY REALLY UNDERSTAND
THEY COULD NOT*

SO FINALLY UPON A RUGGED CROSS
THEY KILLED THE MAN WHO WOULD NOT SUFFER LOSS
AND WHEN AT LAST THEY TOOK WHAT WILLINGLY HE GAVE
HE DIED BUT COULD THEY KEEP HIM IN THE GRAVE

*THEY COULD NOT
THEY COULD NOT
THOUGH THEY TRIED
THEY COULD NOT
AND WHEN AT LAST THEY TOOK FROM HIM
WHAT WILLINGLY HE GAVE
COULD THEY KEEP HIM IN THE GRAVE
COULD THEY KEEP HIM IN THE GRAVE
COULD THEY KEEP HIM IN THE GRAVE*

*THEY COULD NOT
THEY COULD NOT
PRAISE GOD
THEY COULD NOT
AND WHEN AT LAST THEY TOOK FROM HIM
WHAT WILLINGLY HE GAVE
COULD THEY KEEP HIM IN THE GRAVE
THEY COULD NOT
THEY COULD NOT*

IN THE NAME OF THE LORD

by Phill McHugh, Gloria Gaither & Sandi Patti Helvering

CROWDS HAVE LINED THE NARROW STREET
TO SEE THIS MAN FROM GALILEE
JUST A CARPENTER, SOME SAY
LEADING FOOLS ASTRAY
YET MANY KNEEL TO GIVE HIM PRAISE
AND IN HIS EYES THEY GLIMPSE THE POWER
THAT SEES THE HEARTS OF ALL MEN
AND HE KNOWS HIS FATHER'S MIND
HE SPEAKS HIS FATHER'S WORDS
FOR HE COMES *IN THE NAME OF THE LORD*

THERE IS STRENGTH IN THE NAME OF THE LORD
THERE IS POWER IN THE NAME OF THE LORD
THERE IS HOPE IN THE NAME OF THE LORD
BLESSED IS HE WHO COMES IN THE NAME OF THE LORD

WHEN MY PLANS HAVE FALLEN THROUGH
AND WHEN MY STRENGTH IS NEARLY GONE
WHEN THERE'S NOTHING LEFT TO DO
I JUST DEPEND ON YOU
AND THE POWER OF YOUR NAME
AND AS WE CALL UPON YOUR NAME
YOUR STRENGTH THROUGH WEAKNESS TO SHOW
WE CAN KNOW THE MASTER'S PLAN
EXTEND THE MASTER'S HAND
WHEN WE COME *IN THE NAME OF THE LORD*

THERE IS STRENGTH IN THE NAME OF THE LORD
THERE IS POWER IN THE NAME OF THE LORD
THERE IS HOPE IN THE NAME OF THE LORD
BLESSED IS HE WHO COMES IN THE NAME OF THE LORD

HIS NAME WILL BE WORSHIPED FOREVER
CREATOR, REDEEMER AND KING

THERE IS STRENGTH IN THE NAME OF THE LORD
THERE IS POWER IN THE NAME OF THE LORD
AND THERE IS HOPE IN THE NAME OF THE LORD
BLESSED IS HE WHO COMES IN THE NAME OF THE LORD

BLESSED IS HE WHO COMES
BLESSED IS HE WHO COMES
BLESSED IS HE WHO COMES

IN THE NAME OF THE LORD

THE NAME OF THE LORD

"I recently read a book called *LORD, I WANT TO KNOW YOU* by Kay Arthur, which is a study of the names of God. I was so consumed by that book that I would think about it day and night. I would be thinking about it when I was driving in the car, straightening Anna's room, or shopping at the grocery store.

"An interesting thing happened one day when I was going through the produce section of Murphy's Pic-N-Pay. As I was doing my weekly grocery shopping thinking about the names of the Lord, the strength there is in knowing the Lord, what hope there is and what power there is in the name of the Lord, a song came to me. Right there in the produce section of Pic-N-Pay! I think it is a reminder that wherever we are, the Lord speaks to us. Whether we are in church on Sunday, whether it be our daily quiet time with the Lord, or even in the grocery store - the name of the Lord gives us strength, power and hope wherever we are."

SOMEBODY BELIEVED

by Gary Dunham & Rosemary Dunham

ABRAHAM BELIEVED THE LORD
HIS FAITH WAS COUNTED GOOD
AND NOAH BY HIS TRUST WAS LED
TO SAFETY THROUGH THE FLOOD
AND JERICHO WAS CONQUERED
THE GIANT DAVID SLEW
AND ALL BECAUSE THEY TRUSTED IN WHAT GOD COULD DO

SOMEBODY BELIEVED (SOMEBODY BELIEVED)
SOMEBODY BELIEVED (SOMEBODY BELIEVED)
SOMEONE DARED TO TAKE THE GOOD LORD AT HIS WORD
SOMEBODY BELIEVED (SOMEBODY BELIEVED)
SOMEBODY BELIEVED (SOMEBODY BELIEVED)
AND GOD MOVED HIS MIGHTY HAND WHEN **SOMEBODY BELIEVED**

THE SINNER FINDS THE SAVIOR
THE BLIND MAN FINALLY SEES
THE WEAK MAN FINDS HIS STRENGTH
TO CARRY ON
ALL BECAUSE SOMEBODY
SPENT SOME TIME DOWN ON THEIR KNEES
BELIEVIN' THAT IN JESUS EVERY BATTLE CAN BE WON

SOMEBODY BELIEVED (SOMEBODY BELIEVED)
SOMEBODY BELIEVED (SOMEBODY BELIEVED)
SOMEONE DARED TO TAKE THE GOOD LORD AT HIS WORD
SOMEBODY BELIEVED (SOMEBODY BELIEVED)
SOMEBODY BELIEVED (SOMEBODY BELIEVED)
AND GOD MOVED HIS MIGHTY HAND WHEN **SOMEBODY BELIEVED**

ST. PETER WALKED ON THE WATER
THE OTHERS WERE IN SHOCK
HE SAID, "THERE AIN'T NOTHIN' TO IT BOYS
I WAS STANDIN' ON THE ROCK"

SOMEBODY BELIEVED (SOMEBODY BELIEVED)
SOMEBODY BELIEVED (SOMEBODY BELIEVED)
SOMEONE DARED TO TAKE THE GOOD LORD AT HIS WORD
SOMEBODY BELIEVED (SOMEBODY BELIEVED)
SOMEBODY BELIEVED (SOMEBODY BELIEVED)
AND GOD MOVED HIS MIGHTY HAND WHEN **SOMEBODY BELIEVED**
AND GOD MOVED HIS MIGHTY HAND WHEN **SOMEBODY BELIEVED**

SANDI'S SONG

by Sandi Patti Helvering

MY THOUGHTS DON'T COME EASY LIKE THEY USED TO
I WISH I COULD WRITE A SONG FOR YOU
'CAUSE THE WAY I FEEL ABOUT YOU
ONLY A SONG WILL DO
MY LIFE'S TAKEN ON NEW MEANING SINCE YOU CAME ALONG

NOW MY LIFE IS A SONG
SO IT'S WITH THIS SONG I TELL YOU
'CAUSE SOMETIMES SAYIN' "I LOVE YOU" ISN'T ENOUGH
SOME PEOPLE COULD WRITE IT BETTER
BUT THEY'D MISS THE LOVE THAT I HAVE FOR YOU
SO YOU BE THE WORDS AND I'LL BE THE MELODY
THEN WE CAN SING OUR SONG
'CAUSE SOMETIMES I JUST HAVE TO TELL YOU
BUT I DON'T KNOW HOW
THEN I HEARD YOUR WORDS
AND I CAN SING THIS SONG

NOW MY LIFE IS A SONG
SO IT'S WITH THIS SONG I TELL YOU
'CAUSE SOMETIMES SAYIN' "I LOVE YOU" ISN'T ENOUGH
SO YOU BE THE WORDS
AND I'LL BE THE MELODY
WE'LL SING OUR SONG THROUGHOUT ALL ETERNITY
YOU BE THE WORDS
AND I'LL BE THE MELODY
THIS IS MY SONG
AND I'M SINGIN' IT FOR YOU

IT IS WELL WITH MY SOUL

by Philip P. Bliss & Horatio G. Spafford

WHEN PEACE LIKE A RIVER ATTENDETH MY WAY
WHEN SORROWS LIKE SEA BILLOWS ROLL
WHATEVER MY LOT
THOU HAST TAUGHT ME TO SAY IT IS WELL
    IT IS WELL WITH MY SOUL

    IT IS WELL WITH MY SOUL
    IT IS WELL
    IT IS WELL WITH MY SOUL

AND LORD HASTE THE DAY
WHEN MY FAITH SHALL BE SIGHT
THE CLOUDS BE ROLLED BACK AS A SCROLL
THE TRUMP SHALL RESOUND
AND THE LORD SHALL DESCEND
EVEN SO
    IT IS WELL WITH MY SOUL

    IT IS WELL
    IT IS WELL WITH MY SOUL
    IT IS WELL
    IT IS WELL WITH MY SOUL

by Rhea Miller & George Beverly Shea

I'D RATHER HAVE JESUS
THAN SILVER OR GOLD
I'D RATHER BE HIS
THAN HAVE RICHES UNTOLD

I'D RATHER HAVE JESUS
THAN HOUSES OR LAND
I'D RATHER BE LED
BY HIS NAIL PIERCED HAND

I'D RATHER HAVE JESUS
THAN MAN'S APPLAUSE
I'D RATHER BE FAITHFUL
TO HIS DEAR CAUSE
I'D RATHER HAVE JESUS
THAN WORLD-WIDE FAME
I'D RATHER BE TRUE
TO HIS HOLY NAME

THAN TO BE THE KING OF A VAST DOMAIN
OR BE HELD IN SIN'S DREAD SWAY

I'D RATHER HAVE JESUS
THAN ANYTHING
THIS WORLD OFFERS TODAY

I'D RATHER HAVE JESUS

Cradle Song

by Mark Gersmehl

I WATCH BESIDE YOUR CRADLE
YOUR FACE TOUCHED BY THE MOON
MY HEART JUST ACHES AND TREMBLES
WITH ALL MY LOVE FOR YOU

YOUR EYES SHINE LIKE YOUR FATHER'S
THAT NOSE LOOKS JUST LIKE ME
I STARE IN AWE AND WONDER AT SUCH A MYSTERY

HOW GOD CAN TOUCH
THE LOVE OF A MAN AND WIFE
AND BLOSSOM IT
INTO THE BREATH OF LIFE
JUST LOOK AT THIS LIFE

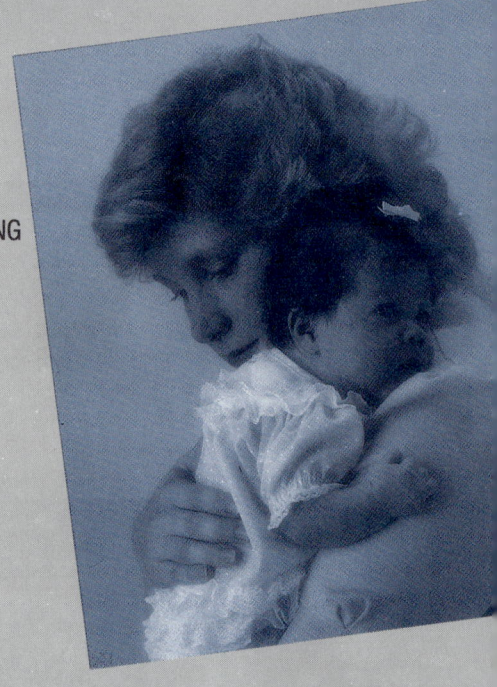

OUR EYES ARE FILLED WITH DREAMING
WE WANT SO MUCH FOR YOU
BUT WE MIGHT FAIL YOU OFTEN
BEFORE YOUR LIFE IS THROUGH

ONLY YOUR HEAVENLY FATHER
CAN HEAR YOUR EVERY PRAYER
WHEN WE ARE JUST A MEMORY
YOUR LORD WILL STILL BE THERE

SO ON OUR KNEES
WE PRAY THIS *CRADLE SONG*
THAT YOU'LL ALWAYS KNOW
THE LORD WILL KEEP YOU STRONG
WE WANT YOU TO UNDERSTAND
YOU REST IN HIS LOVING HANDS
FOR YOU ARE JESUS' LITTLE LAMB

HOSANNA

By Billy Smiley & Mark Gersmehl

HAVE YOU HEARD THE STORY
THE CHRIST IS FINALLY HERE
HE'S AT THE EDGE OF THE CITY
LET'S RUN
I'VE JUST GOTTA BE NEAR HIM
ALL THE PEOPLE ARE SHOUTING
THEY'VE COME JUST TO SEE THEIR KING
TELL THE DAUGHTER OF ZION
REJOICE, FOR WE'VE BEEN REDEEMED
HE IS RIDING VICTORIOUS
LIKE THE PROPHETS FORETOLD
VISIONS ARE GLORIOUS
WE MUST BOW DOWN BEFORE HIM
LAY OUR HEARTS AND SOULS BEFORE HIM
LORD OF ALL

HOSANNA, HOSANNA
SEE HIM RIDE IN MAJESTY
HOSANNA, HOSANNA
LORD OF ALL ETERNITY
HOSANNA, HOSANNA
RAISE YOUR HANDS IN VICTORY
HOSANNA, HOSANNA
HE'S COME TO SET HIS PEOPLE FREE

BEHOLD YOUR SALVATION
HE COMES TO THE WILLING HEARTS
BLESSED OVER ALL NATIONS
HIS LOVE WILL NEVER DEPART
NOW HE'S REIGNING VICTORIOUS
FOREVER HE IS LORD
IS LORD
CHRIST HAS DELIVERED US
WE MUST FALL DOWN BEFORE HIM
LAY OUR HEARTS AND SOULS BEFORE HIM
LORD OF ALL

HOSANNA, HOSANNA
SEE HIM RIDE IN MAJESTY
HOSANNA, HOSANNA
LORD OF ALL ETERNITY
HOSANNA, HOSANNA
RAISE YOUR HANDS IN VICTORY
HOSANNA, HOSANNA
HE'S COME TO SET HIS PEOPLE FREE

HE'S COME TO SET HIS PEOPLE FREE
HE'S COME TO SET HIS PEOPLE FREE

LOVE IN ANY LANGUAGE

by Jon Mohr & John Mays

JE T'AIME
TE AMO
YA TYIBYA LYUBLYU
ANI-OHEVET-OTHKA
I LOVE YOU
THE SOUNDS ARE ALL AS DIFFERENT
AS THE LANDS FROM WHICH THEY CAME
AND THOUGH OUR WORDS ARE ALL UNIQUE
OUR HEARTS ARE STILL THE SAME

LOVE IN ANY LANGUAGE
STRAIGHT FROM THE HEART
PULLS US ALL TOGETHER
NEVER APART
AND ONCE WE LEARN TO SPEAK IT
ALL THE WORLD WILL HEAR
LOVE IN ANY LANGUAGE
FLUENTLY SPOKEN HERE

WE TEACH THE YOUNG OUR DIFFERENCES
YET LOOK HOW WE'RE THE SAME
WE LOVE TO LAUGH
WE DREAM OUR DREAMS
WE KNOW THE STING OF PAIN
FROM LENNINGRAD TO LEXINGTON
THE FARMER LOVES HIS LAND
AND DADDIES ALL GET MISTY-EYED
TO GIVE THEIR DAUGHTER'S HAND

OH MAYBE WHEN WE REALIZE
HOW MUCH THERE IS TO SHARE
WE'LL FIND TOO MUCH IN COMMON
TO PRETEND IT ISN'T THERE

LOVE IN ANY LANGUAGE
STRAIGHT FROM THE HEART
PULLS US ALL TOGETHER
NEVER APART
AND ONCE WE LEARN TO SPEAK IT
ALL THE WORLD WILL HEAR
LOVE IN ANY LANGUAGE
FLUENTLY SPOKEN HERE

THOUGH THE RHETORIC OF GOVERNMENTS
MAY KEEP US WORLDS APART
THERE'S NO MISINTERPRETING
THE LANGUAGE OF THE HEART

LOVE IN ANY LANGUAGE FLUENTLY SPOKEN HERE
LOVE IN ANY LANGUAGE FLUENTLY SPOKEN HERE

It's Your Song, Lord

by Sandi Patti Helvering, Billy Smiley & Claire Cloninger

IT'S YOUR SONG, LORD
YOU CREATED THE GIFT THAT WE BRING
IT'S YOUR SONG, LORD
YOU CREATED MUSIC SO WE COULD SING

IT'S A REALLY GOOD NIGHT TO BE PRAISING YOUR NAME
THIS PLACE IS SO FULL OF YOUR LIGHT
AND I THANK YOU FOR SISTERS AND BROTHERS LIKE THESE
AND THE SONG THAT WE'RE SINGING TONIGHT

'CAUSE IT'S YOUR SONG, LORD
YOU CREATED THE GIFT THAT WE BRING
IT'S YOUR SONG, LORD
YOU CREATED MUSIC SO WE COULD SING
SO WE'LL SEND THE MELODY RIGHT BACK AROUND
AND MAKE A PERFECT CIRCLE WITH THE SOUND
WE LOVE TO LIFT OUR VOICES, LORD
'CAUSE EVERY TIME WE DO
WE'RE SINGING YOUR SONG FOR YOU

WHEN WE COME TOGETHER, IT'S ALWAYS THE SAME
THE LOVE IN OUR HEARTS IS SO STRONG
AND WE'RE LONGING TO TELL YOU AND PRAISE YOU AGAIN
SO THANK YOU FOR SENDING THE SONG

'CAUSE IT'S YOUR SONG, LORD
YOU CREATED THE GIFT THAT WE BRING
IT'S YOUR SONG, LORD
YOU CREATED MUSIC SO WE COULD SING
SO WE'LL SEND THE MELODY RIGHT BACK AROUND
AND MAKE A PERFECT CIRCLE WITH THE SOUND
WE LOVE TO LIFT OUR VOICES, LORD
"CAUSE EVERY TIME WE DO
WE'RE SINGING YOUR SONG FOR YOU

IN THE TUNE OF THE RAINDROPS
IN THE SONG OF THE WIND
ALL MUSIC BEGINS IN YOUR HEART
WHEN WE LIFT A SONG
WE'RE JUST SENDING IT HOME
BACK TO WHERE IT STARTS

'CAUSE IT'S YOUR SONG, LORD
YOU CREATED THE GIFT THAT WE BRING
IT'S YOUR SONG, LORD
YOU CREATED MUSIC SO WE COULD SING
SO WE'LL SEND THE MELODY RIGHT BACK AROUND
AND MAKE A PERFECT CIRCLE WITH THE SOUND
WE LOVE TO LIFT OUR VOICES, LORD
'CAUSE EVERY TIME WE DO
WE'RE SINGING YOUR SONG
SINGING YOUR SONG
SINGING YOUR SONG FOR YOU

SHINE DOWN

by Billy Smiley, Mark Gersmehl & Bob Farrell

SHINE DOWN YOUR LIGHT ON ME
LET THE PEOPLE SEE
IN YOUR PRESENCE DARKNESS FLEES
FATHER OF LIGHT
SHINE DOWN ON ME
SHINE DOWN YOUR LIGHT ON ME
LET THE PEOPLE SEE
IN YOUR PRESENCE DARKNESS FLEES
FATHER OF LIGHT SHINE DOWN ON ME

THERE'S A LAND FULL OF GLORY
IN A PLACE WHERE THERE IS NO NIGHT
AND IN THAT HOLY CITY
BURNS THE BEACON OF EVERLASTING LIGHT
THE LIGHT THAT KEEPS REACHING
TO THE PEOPLE OF EVERY LAND
A LOVE THAT IS LONGING
TO FILL THE HEART OF EVERY MAN

SHINE DOWN YOUR LIGHT ON ME
LET THE PEOPLE SEE
THAT IN YOUR PRESENCE DARKNESS FLEES
FATHER OF LIGHT
SHINE DOWN ON ME
SHINE DOWN YOUR LIGHT ON ME
LET THE PEOPLE SEE
THAT IN YOUR PRESENCE DARKNESS FLEES
FATHER OF LIGHT SHINE DOWN ON ME

THERE'S NO SUN IN THAT CITY
THE FATHER'S THRONE IS IT'S ONLY LIGHT
THE LAMP OF SALVATION
THE HOPE THAT IS ALWAYS GLOWING BRIGHT

IT SCATTERS THE DARKNESS
SWEPT AWAY BY HIS MIGHTY HAND
NOW ALL THE NATIONS CAN WORSHIP
SING THE SONG OF THAT GLORIOUS LAMB

SHINE DOWN YOUR LIGHT ON ME
LET THE PEOPLE SEE
THAT IN YOUR PRESENCE DARKNESS FLEES
FATHER OF LIGHT
SHINE DOWN ON ME

SHINE DOWN YOUR LIGHT ON ME
LET THE PEOPLE SEE
THAT IN YOUR PRESENCE DARKNESS FLEES
FATHER OF LIGHT SHINE DOWN ON ME

WAS IT A MORNING LIKE THIS

by Jim Croegaert

WAS IT A MORNING LIKE THIS
WHEN THE SON STILL HID FROM JERUSALEM
AND MARY ROSE FROM HER BED
TO TEND THE LORD SHE THOUGHT WAS DEAD

WAS IT A MORNING LIKE THIS
WHEN MARY WALKED DOWN FROM JERUSALEM
AND TWO ANGELS STOOD AT THE TOMB
BEARERS OF NEWS SHE WOULD HEAR SOON

DID THE GRASS SING
DID THE EARTH REJOICE TO FEEL YOU AGAIN

OVER AND OVER LIKE A TRUMPET UNDERGROUND
DID THE EARTH SEEM TO POUND, "HE IS RISEN"
OVER AND OVER IN A NEVER-ENDING ROUND
"HE IS RISEN, ALLELUIA, ALLELUIA"

WAS IT A MORNING LIKE THIS
WHEN PETER AND JOHN RAN FROM JERUSALEM
AND AS THEY RACED TOWARD THE TOMB
BENEATH THEIR FEET WAS THERE A TUNE

DID THE GRASS SING
DID THE EARTH REJOICE TO FEEL YOU AGAIN

OVER AND OVER LIKE A TRUMPET UNDERGROUND
DID THE EARTH SEEM TO POUND, "HE IS RISEN"
OVER AND OVER IN A NEVER-ENDING ROUND
"HE IS RISEN, ALLELUIA, ALLELUIA"

WAS IT A MORNING LIKE THIS
WHEN MY LORD LOOKED OUT ON JERUSALEM
"HE IS RISEN, ALLELUIA, ALLELUIA, ALLELUIA"

WHEN THE TIME COMES

by Dave Kavich

CLEANSE ME LORD
OF ALL MY SILLY, SAD CHARADES
HOW I WANT TO BE
ALL AND ONLY YOURS
TAKE AWAY THE CLUTTER
IN MY LIFE EVERYDAY
AND MAKE ME LIKE A CHILD AT PLAY

GIVE ME JOY
I LOVE TO LAUGH AND CRY WITH YOU
YOU'VE BECOME A FRIEND
WITH ME ALL THE TIME
HELP ME TO BE PATIENT
AS I WATCH AND AS I PRAY
GROWING IN YOUR LOVE EACH DAY
LORD SHOW ME THE WAY

**WHEN THE TIME COMES
I WANT HIM TO KNOW ME
WHEN THE TIME COMES
I WANT TO BE THERE
WHEN THE TIME COMES
I WANNA BE READY
WHEN JESUS COMES TO TAKE ME
TAKE ME HOME**

FILL ME LORD
I WANT YOUR LOVE TO OVERFLOW
RUNNING FREE THROUGH ME
TO A LONELY WORLD
LET ME SHARE THAT SIMPLE TRUTH
THAT SETS PEOPLE FREE
HOW I WANT THEM ALL TO SEE HOW IT CAN BE

**WHEN THE TIME COMES
I WANT HIM TO KNOW ME
WHEN THE TIME COMES
I WANT TO BE THERE
WHEN THE TIME COMES
I WANNA BE READY
WHEN JESUS COMES TO TAKE ME
TAKE ME HOME**

YES, GOD IS REAL

by Kenneth Morris

I CANNOT TELL JUST HOW YOU FELT
WHEN JESUS TOOK ALL YOUR SINS AWAY
BUT SINCE THAT DAY AND SINCE THAT VERY HOUR
YES, GOD'S REAL FOR I CAN FEEL HIS HOLY POWER

NOW THERE ARE SOME THINGS THAT I MAY NOT KNOW
AND THERE ARE SOME PLACES THAT I CANNOT GO
BUT I AM SURE OF THIS ONE THING
THAT MY GOD IS REAL AND I CAN FEEL HIM DEEP WITHIN

OH YES, GOD IS REAL
HE'S VERY REAL IN MY SOUL
OH YES, GOD IS REAL
FOR HE HAS WASHED AND MADE ME WHOLE
AND HIS LOVE FOR ME IS LIKE PURE GOLD
YES, GOD IS REAL FOR I CAN FEEL HIM IN MY SOUL

WE SHALL BEHOLD HIM

by Dottie Rambo

THE SKY SHALL UNFOLD
PREPARING HIS ENTRANCE
THE STARS SHALL APPLAUD HIM
WITH THUNDERS OF PRAISE
THE SWEET LIGHT IN HIS EYES
SHALL ENHANCE THOSE AWAITING
AND WE SHALL BEHOLD HIM
THEN FACE TO FACE

OH, WE SHALL BEHOLD HIM
WE SHALL BEHOLD HIM
FACE TO FACE IN ALL OF HIS GLORY
OH, WE SHALL BEHOLD HIM
YES, WE SHALL BEHOLD HIM
FACE TO FACE OUR SAVIOR AND LORD

THE ANGELS SHALL SOUND
THE SHOUT OF HIS COMING
THE SLEEPING SHALL RISE
FROM THEIR SLUMBERING PLACE
AND THOSE WHO REMAIN
SHALL BE CHANGED IN A MOMENT
AND WE SHALL BEHOLD HIM
THEN FACE TO FACE

WE SHALL BEHOLD HIM
OH YES, WE SHALL BEHOLD HIM
FACE TO FACE IN ALL OF HIS GLORY
WE SHALL BEHOLD HIM
OH YES, WE SHALL BEHOLD HIM
FACE TO FACE MY SAVIOR AND LORD
AND WE SHALL BEHOLD HIM
OUR SAVIOR AND LORD
SAVIOR AND LORD

GLORIOUS MORNING

by Gary McSpadden, Lari Goss & Linda Dooley

OVER THE HILLSIDE, THE SUNRISE IS COMING
GENTLE AND WARM, IT WAKES UP THE DAY
REFLECTING HIS LIGHT FOR JESUS HAS RISEN
HEAVEN AND EARTH NOW JOIN IN THE PRAISE
THOSE WHO HAVE SEEN HIM NOW ARE BELIEVERS
AND WE WHO NOW BY BELIEVING HAVE SEEN
LIFTING OUR VOICES IN ONE MIGHTY CHORUS
JESUS IS LORD AND SAVIOUR AND KING

GLORIOUS MORNING JESUS IS RISEN
NO TOMB COULD HOLD HIM NO STONE COULD SEAL
GLORIOUS MORNING THE WORLD HAS A SAVIOUR
HE IS ALIVE AND HIS TRUTH IS REVEALED

ETERNITY'S WAR FOUGHT THROUGH THE AGES
COMES TO AN END AT CALVARY'S CROSS
AND THE TOMB NOW IS EMPTY
LIGHT SHATTERS THE DARKNESS
NIGHT THAT SEEMED ENDLESS GIVES WAY TO THE DAWN

OH, GLORIOUS MORNING JESUS IS RISEN
NO TOMB COULD HOLD HIM NO STONE COULD SEAL
GLORIOUS MORNING THE WORLD HAS A SAVIOUR
HE IS ALIVE AND HIS TRUTH IS REVEALED

GLORIOUS MORNING JESUS IS RISEN
NO TOMB COULD HOLD HIM NO STONE COULD SEAL
GLORIOUS MORNING THE WORLD HAS A SAVIOUR
HE IS ALIVE AND HIS TRUTH IS REVEALED
GLORIOUS MORNING

IN HIS HAND

by Gary Chapman & Michael W. Smith

I'VE HAD DISAPPOINTMENTS
AND SO HAVE YOU
I REMEMBER TIMES WHEN TIMES WERE BAD
BUT I AM SO GLAD
FOR EVERY MOMENT
THAT I'VE SPENT IN HIS HAND
IN HIS HAND

IN HIS HAND
THERE'S ONLY SAFETY
NOTHING THERE CAN TOUCH YOU EXCEPT HIM
BRING YOUR BURDENS
AND ALL YOUR FAILURES
LAY THEM DOWN AND REST HERE IN HIS HAND

I WILL HAVE MORE PROBLEMS
AND SO WILL YOU
BUT THROUGH EVERY ONE WE ALL CAN STAND
IF WE'RE IN HIS HAND
SO ARE THE TRIALS
THERE IS NO CAUSE FOR FEAR
IN HIS HAND

IN HIS HAND
THERE'S ONLY SAFETY
NOTHING THERE CAN TOUCH YOU EXCEPT HIM
BRING YOUR BURDENS
AND ALL YOUR FAILURES
LAY THEM DOWN AND REST HERE IN HIS HAND

A BRIGHT LIGHT TO A DARK WORLD

by KELLY DeLANEY

"She's a personality who is a bright light to a dark world." That's how Greg Nelson describes the effect of Sandi Patti and her music on all who hear her sing.

Nelson has been Sandi's record producer since 1982. "She brings a spiritual consciousness to people when she's around them," he continues. "People who are not necessarily lovers of inspirational music appreciate her talent, so she is able to minister to those people, too."

Nelson, whose production credits also include: Joe English, Steve Green, Connie Scott, David Meece, Scott Wesley Brown, Bonnie Bramlett, and Larnelle Harris, among others, terms his first project with Sandi a "learning experience". That album, *Lift Up The Lord*, earned a Dove Award in 1983 from the Gospel Music Associaton, for Inspirational Album of the Year. It also received a Grammy nomination for best Gospel Performance - Contemporary.

"My way of doing things (producing records) was more of a spur of the moment, head session way of doing it," Nelson adds. "But, she, on the other hand, was more used to things being approached in an orchestral way."

By the next year when it was time to record Sandi's live album, *More Than Wonderful*, Nelson was able to build upon his first production experience with Sandi. "I understood where she was coming from," he explains. "When we did *More Than Wonderful*, something wonderful really did happen; it clicked."

The title song from that album, a duet with Larnelle Harris, was a Grammy Award winning tune in 1984 for Best Gospel Performance Duo or Group. It also took top honors at the Gospel Music Association's Dove Awards that year as Song of the Year. The album, in addition to winning a Dove Award as Inspirational Album of the Year, also earned Sandi and Nelson a Dove Award as co-producers.

"Sandi was very instrumental in selecting the songs for that album," **Nelson** notes. He adds that Sandi has a reputation of carefully choosing material to record. "One of her many strengths is that she is a bear for the lyric," he says. "She'll spend days thinking, 'Now did Jesus (in 'Via Dolorosa') walk *to* the heart of Jerusalem or *through* the heart?' She'll sit and think of those little words and if it's right."

When Sandi and Nelson listen for songs to record, they try to find tunes which have worth and say things they feel people need to hear. "We look for strong ideas, strong statements that are well done and aren't said the same way," he says. "For example, 'Via Dolorosa' is not like any other song. It has a great concept. 'Upon This Rock' is a great idea - that's what we look for."

Nelson feels that Sandi possesses a captivating quality which is only enhanced through the sincerity of her music. "One of the things which draws people to her is that she is a down to earth girl," "She has tremendous talent, but if you remove that talent, you've got a vulnerable, down to earth girl who is not afraid to show everything - this is where I am - and people relate to that. There is an innate believability about her because she is just what she is. I think that's what people want; you can't force believability."

Together, Sandi and Nelson have won a stack of awards for the music they've recorded. More importantly they have teamed up to touch people's lives.

It has been a working relationship Nelson cherishes. "I look forward to working with all my artists because each one is special," **Nelson** says. "I get excited about working with Sandi because you know it's going to be good."

Indeed it is. The proof is in the music

The lights dimmed. The singer placed her microphone on its stand and stood motionless as the orchestra began the familiar introduction. There was a hush that fell over the audience as, softly, her clear voice began: "The sky shall unfold, preparing His entrance..." But it was not "The Voice" (as ad writers once labeled her) that caused the hush. It was her face, her hands, her whole being that was spelling out to us what voices and words could never say. Suddenly eight-thousand persons were experiencing what no mortal has *ever* experienced: the appearance of the long-awaited Messiah. The "sky was unfolding," "the sleeping" were rising "from their slumbering place". We felt it. The singer was not just telling *about* a Biblically prophesied event; she was transporting us into the experience itself with a story, and she was not only the storyteller, she was becoming the "story" herself.

As she reached the climactic last chorus: "We shall behold Him," the spotlights slowly moved from the singer and her descriptive motions to focus, instead, on a group of about one-hundred individuals in the audience who now spontaneously rose to their feet. All one-hundred of them were mirroring the singer's hand movements. These were, we gradually came to realize, a "choir" of the hearing impaired. Yes! and they were "singing along"!

Perhaps this experience, better than any other, illustrates the tremendous power to communicate that is a part of Sandi Patti. More than the words, more than the music, more than "The Voice", is the Message, the love for people, and the deep desire to say something meaningful to them. This is the special charisma of Sandi, the artist.

As for me, a songwriter, there is no greater fulfillment than to create a lyric I believe can change a person's life, and then have that lyric communicated (not just sung, but communicated!) by an artist like Sandi, who not only understands, but makes sure with everything she is that her audience understands, too. Yes, Sandi Patti is more than "The Voice," and what she sings is more than music!

MORE THAN MUSIC

by GLORIA GAITHER